The Merit System
and Municipal
Civil Service

Recent Titles in
Contributions in Political Science
Series Editor: Bernard K. Johnpoll

THE MERIT SYSTEM AND MUNICIPAL CIVIL SERVICE

A Fostering of Social Inequality

FRANCES GOTTFRIED

CONTRIBUTIONS IN POLITICAL SCIENCE, NUMBER 201

Greenwood Press
NEW YORK • WESTPORT, CONNECTICUT • LONDON

Library of Congress Cataloging-in-Publication Data

Gottfried, Frances.
  The merit system and municipal civil service.

  (Contributions in political science, ISSN 0147–1066 ;
no. 201)
    Bibliography: p.
    Includes index.
    1. Municipal officials and employees—United States.
  2. Affirmative action programs—United States.
  3. Civil service—United States—Minority employment.
  4. Women in the civil service—United States.   5. Civil
  service reform—United States.   6. Social justice.
  7. Equality—United States. I. Title.   II. Series.
  JS358.G597 1988   352'.0056'0973   87–23759
  ISBN 0–313–25741–8 (lib. bdg. : alk. paper)

British Library Cataloguing in Publication Data is available.

Library of Congress Catalog Card Number: 87–23759
ISBN: 0–313–25741–8
ISSN: 0147–1066

First published in 1988

Greenwood Press, Inc.
88 Post Road West, Westport, Connecticut 06881

Printed in the United States of America

The paper used in this book complies with the
Permanent Paper Standard issued by the National
Information Standards Organization (Z39.48–1984).

10   9   8   7   6   5   4   3   2   1

To my Mother,
Jean Gottfried

Contents

    Employment Programs   117

6. Conclusions   151

    Selected Bibliography   163

    Index   175

Tables

Acknowledgments

To my friend and colleague, Professor Marilyn Gittell of the City University of New York, I am deeply grateful for her assistance in the conceptualization of this study, for her invaluable criticisms and suggestions, and for setting a standard of scholarship and social commitment that I hope this book begins to approach. I am most appreciative of the help of Professor James T. Crown of New York University, who critiqued the draft of this work, and for his many years of encouragement toward the completion of the study. I would like to thank Arnold J. Gould for his helpful comments and suggestions in the collection of legal research for Chapter 4, and his strong moral support during the long year in which I wrote this study. In addition, I am much indebted to Anne Goldstein, who contributed her professional expertise in the typing of this manuscript.

To my mother, Jean Gottfried, I dedicate this book, not only for her tremendous support on this project, but for a lifetime of encouragement and support that she has given me.

Introduction

This book examines the hypothesis that the rigid structure of municipal civil service systems and the principle of meritocracy underlying that system have contributed to and maintained a system of social inequity in the public service, and that such values as representation and responsive service delivery are secondary to the protection of professional power and control.

The study analyzes legislative, judicial, and administrative efforts that attempted to make municipal civil service systems more equitable. Existing personnel systems and controls exercised by unions and professional groups are also evaluated with regard to their efforts to constrain change. Efforts to effect change in municipal civil service systems are important because, as the United States moved from an industrial to a service society, more services have been demanded of government, and there has been a steady growth of the state and local government workforces. This appears to be the long-term trend, despite recent cutbacks in city personnel and services.[1] As such, it may be argued that the public service should offer the greatest opportunity for entrance of minorities and women who have been excluded from government employment. This, however, has not been the case. The reason for the inability of the public service to adapt to the needs of these groups may be attributed to the rigid structure of the civil service system.

My concern is with the intent and implementation of public policy. Most of the literature dealing with employment programs is the work of economists rather than political scientists.[2] As a result, most of the studies are concerned with impact on employment, the workforce, or the economy, rather than public policy. This study focuses on how policy is made and attempts to identify, for example, major sources of power in policy making and to what degree the growth of government has shifted the task of policy making from politicians to professional technocrats.[3] In this context it is important to examine attitudes and opinions regarding civil service systems by those individuals who are responsible for implementation.

The civil service (or merit) system was created "both to insure that competent employees are chosen and to prevent parties, or political figures, from offering patronage as a means of gaining votes or other political advantage."[4] The merit system was an outgrowth of the "good government" movement and was characterized as a recruitment system based on competitive examinations, relative security of tenure, and political neutrality.[5] Its supporters believed that these procedures would guarantee recruitment on the basis of objective measures of competence, and that an open system would exist. They also assumed that political commitments would be eliminated as a *sine qua non* for employment.

Early studies of public administration called for the separation of public administration from politics.[6] By the time that Leonard White wrote the first text on public administration in 1926, it was assumed that public servants were completely separate from politics.[7] This belief was held until World War II, when Paul Appleby presented a thesis antithetical to the politics and administration dichotomy. Appleby suggested that all administration and policy making in government are political.[8]

When the civil service reformers drafted the Pendleton Act of 1883, their interest was in developing a civil service system free of political manipulation and in an efficient personnel system void of discriminatory procedures in the selection process.[9] This study attempts to demonstrate that professionals politically manipulate the civil service system at the current time.

Concurrent with the development of the civil service reform movement, a second movement originating in the private sector had begun. This was the scientific management movement, whose chief proponent, Frederick W. Taylor, called for efficiency and economy in the goals of administrative systems. As a result of this movement personnel systems began focusing on quantifiable and formal processes, such as written examinations, uniform salary plans, and other new management techniques.[10]

While the civil service reform movement and the scientific management movement began with different purposes, they have developed into a conceptual foundation for modern public administration.[11] Frederick Mosher, however, believes that for the elected officials, appointed administrators, and political scientists, "The policy-administration dichotomy is a convenient crutch, or myth, to support and justify their current status."[12]

The traditional model of public administration, however, has come under attack, and demand has grown for a New Public Administration. This attack emanated from two camps. On one side were the organization theorists, who challenged the foundations of public administration, particularly its assertions of efficiency and political neutrality. On the other side were the political activists, who challenged the basic underpinnings of government institutions, which they claimed to be undemocratic and nonrepresentative.[13] This study will focus on the notions of equity and representativeness as aspects of democracy in municipal civil service systems.

In setting out to examine the hypothesis of this book, that the rigid structure of municipal civil service systems and the principle of meritocracy underlying that system have contributed to and maintained a system of social inequity, it is useful to outline several of the major research questions in the study. There continues to be an assumption that civil service reform was "good." What difference has it made? While the civil service system was designed to produce responsive delivery of services and social equity, it did neither. When the standards for staffing and administering the civil service are determined by professionals whose ideologies and value structures run counter to the interests of the communities being served by these professionals, the result may be unsatisfactory delivery of services to these communities. Although the potential conflict of professional interest versus community interest is always present, it is most acute when the communities in question are severely underrepresented in the professional ranks. What happened when attempts were made to make the system more equitable? The practices and procedures in municipal civil service systems, particularly those aspects of the system relating to qualifications, examinations, and promotions, present institutional barriers which have an exclusionary impact on minorities and women in their pursuit of successful careers in the civil service. Despite the rigid structure of municipal civil service systems, is it possible to make the system more equitable?

The next five chapters contain the elements that examine the hypothesis of the study. Chapter 1 attempts to demonstrate that the patronage system and the spoils system provided a degree of social equity while the civil service reform movement, which was an attempt to rid the society of the evils of patronage and spoils through rigid qualifications and examinations of a merit system, raised new questions of credentialling and quality. The chapter challenges the myth that meritocracy exists in civil service and demonstrates, theoretically, the compatibility of quality and social equity.

Chapter 2 analyzes current practices and procedures in municipal civil service systems with an emphasis on who has power in civil service decision making. Participants analyzed include personnel directors and civil service commissions, professional organizations, municipal unions, and city mayors. The credentialling system will also be examined to determine its impact on the civil service system.

Chapters 3, 4, and 5 examine the impact of attempts at reforming the civil service system. In viewing affirmative action programs, court cases, and public employment programs, the study focuses on the administrative, judicial, and legislative efforts to make the system more equitable. The concept of representation is examined throughout these chapters to determine if minorities and women are represented in the public service based upon their respective numbers in the population in a given

Introduction xvii

locality. A concluding chapter reviews the research presented and assesses the validity of the hypothesis that the rigid structure of municipal civil service and the principle of meritocracy underlying that system have contributed to and maintained a system of social inequity in the public service.

NOTES

1. The local government workforce in the United States, for example, increased by approximately 81 percent between 1964 and 1980. See U.S. Department of Labor, *Employment and Earnings, United States, 1909–78*, Bulletin 1312–11, 1979; *Supplement to Employment and Earnings Revised Establishment Data*, June 1982; and "Employment and Earnings," Table B–2, various months, in Charles L. Betsey, "Minority Participation in the Public Sector" (Washington, D.C.: The Urban Institute, November 1982), p. 5. (Mimeographed paper.)

2. Sar Levitan of the National Manpower Task Force, Bennett Harrison of the Massachusetts Institute of Technology, and Helen Ginsburg at the Center for Studies in Income Maintenance Policy at the New York University School of Social Work are a few of the economists in the country who have been researching employment programs.

3. See Charles E. Lindblom, *The Policy-Making Process* (Englewood Cliffs, N.J.: Prentice-Hall, 1968).

4. Edward C. Banfield and James Q. Wilson, *City Politics* (New York: Vintage Books, 1963), p. 207.

5. Paul P. Van Riper, *History of the United States Civil Service* (Evanston, Ill.: Row, Peterson and Company, 1958), p. 100.

6. See Woodrow Wilson, "The Study of Administration," *Political Science Quarterly* 2 (June 1887): 197–222; Frank J. Goodnow, *Politics and Administration: A Study in Government* (New York: The MacMillan Company, 1900; reprint ed., New York: Russell and Russell, 1967); W. F. Willoughby, *Principles of Public Administration* (Baltimore: Johns Hopkins Press, 1927); and Lewis Mayers, *The Federal Service: A Study of the System of Personnel Administration of the United States Government* (New York: D. Appleton and Company, 1922), pp. 19–25.

7. Leonard D. White, *Introduction to the Study of Public Administration* (New York: The MacMillan Company, 1926; 4th ed., 1955).

8. Paul H. Appleby, *Policy and Administration* (University, Ala.: University of Alabama Press, 1949), pp. 47, 64.

9. Laurence J. O'Toole, Jr., "Doctrines and Developments: Separation of Powers, the Politics-Administration Dichotomy, and the Rise

of the Administrative State," *Public Administration Review* 47 (January/February 1987): 19.

10. Jean J. Couturier, "Court Attacks on Testing: Death Knell or Salvation for Civil Service Systems?" *Good Government*, Winter 1971, p. 11.

11. Joseph P. Viteritti, *Bureaucracy and Social Justice: The Allocation of Jobs and Services to Minority Groups* (Port Washington, N.Y.: Kennikat Press, 1979), p. 33.

12. Frederick C. Mosher, *Democracy and the Public Service*, 2nd ed. (New York: Oxford University Press, 1982), p. 8.

13. Viteritti, *Bureaucracy and Social Justice*, p. 8; for a more extensive discussion of the New Public Administration see Vincent Ostrom, *The Intellectual Crisis in American Public Administration* (University, Ala.: The University of Alabama Press, 1973); Emmette S. Redford, *Democracy in the Administrative State* (New York: Oxford University Press, 1969); and David H. Rosenbloom, "Public Administrative Theory and the Separation of Powers," *Public Administration Review* 43 (May/June 1983): 219–227.

Roots of Municipal Civil Service: The Notion of Meritocracy 1

The civil service (or merit) system was created both to ensure that qualified employees are selected and to prevent political parties or bosses from exchanging patronage for votes or other political advantage.[1] Reformers in urban government characterized the "new structure of municipal government as more moral, more rational, and more efficient and, because it was so, self-evidently more desirable."[2]

In order to understand the discriminatory aspects of the present civil service system, which was established to undermine the patronage system, it is necessary first to locate the system's roots in the patronage and spoils systems, and in the civil service reform movement that emerged in this country during the latter half of the nineteenth century.

It is also essential to focus on the notion of meritocracy in which technical expertise and higher education underlie the rationale for differences in position and income.[3] Under the merit system, particularly as it developed its own procedures and screening devices, only those who had achieved a certain level of education were eligible for jobs. The principle of social equity was almost immediately abandoned under the merit system. In contrast, the patronage system encompassed recruitment procedures which allowed for a cross-section of the population to enter public service without regard to level of education achieved. What emerged was a theory and practice of meritocracy that assumed that the best candidates were those who were most literate and most learned.[4]

PATRONAGE SYSTEM AND SPOILS SYSTEM

Prior to the nineteenth century most civil servants were appointed on a political basis. Most public employees were selected on the basis of political affiliation or family status rather than intelligence or competence to do the job. This characterizes the patronage system in contrast to the merit system. However, the merit system is not necessarily more quality-oriented than the patronage system. Further, the patronage system is not synonymous with a spoils system, which involves greater personal and partisan politics.[5]

The appointment system known as the spoils system flourished with the development of democracy. Frequent elections encouraged politicians to build organizations to influence voters. Their most likely support was from local, state, and federal employees, individuals whose jobs depended on politicians. These appointees could be counted on to support politicians with time and money in future political battles. Frequent elections, however, meant frequent changes. The spoils system rested on three principles: "appointment primarily for political considerations, congressional dictation of most appointments, and rotation of office-holders."[6]

The spoils system reflected an ideological change in the government of the United States. With the election of Andrew Jackson, "egalitarianism, which had been used as a tenet of the new government, became a reality."[7]

Arthur Schlesinger, Jr., suggests that the notion of rotation-in-office was to a large extent thought of as "a sincere measure of reform." The idea of rotation was conceived as a part of a democratic plan to preserve equality of opportunity. The spoils system, despite its faults, effectuated a shift in offices by a class "which could not govern," to an energetic group focusing on public needs. The historical significance of the spoils system, despite whatever evils it brought into American life, was to provide a greater voice in government by the people as a result of increasing popular participation in the government workforce.[8]

The egalitarian momentum behind the spoils system did not prove effective in sustaining popular direction and control of government. Though Jackson and his successors shifted the control of the public service arena from the old aristocracy to the "common people," the national administration was little more accountable to the people as a whole at the close of the nineteenth century than it had been at the close of the eighteenth century. Mosher suggests,

We had effectively though not completely transferred governmental power from one group (the gentry) to another (the politicians); in the process, we suffered a considerable degradation of public office and widespread corruption. We also planted the seeds for a kind of civil service reform quite different from that instituted by Andrew Jackson.[9]

BOSSES AND THE POLITICAL MACHINE

Contemporary political science characterizes American cities in the late nineteenth and early twentieth centuries as being dominated by the political machine. Exercising control during this era was the political boss.[10]

Following the Civil War, American cities experienced rapid population growth as a result of people moving from rural areas, an influx of immigrants, and the new mobility created by railroads.[11] The boss or other party representatives served as a liaison between "the new city dweller" and society. Party politics played a critical role in the city. The party became the focus of such necessities of life as employment and health services; it dispersed its patronage through the local precinct captain. In response, the individual was expected to pay back these favors with party loyalty, as well as a vote on election day. The essential components of the citywide machine headed by the boss were the local neighborhoods.[12]

Thus, the machine was "a primitive network" which provided

a link from the "boss" to both the upper and lower class of cities. "To the upper classes, the boss supplied utility and street car franchises, construction contracts, and other juicy patronage plums."[13] To the new immigrants, the boss served a social welfare function.

One could argue that the major objective of a patronage system is a more responsive bureaucracy. Jackson would argue that it was "the patronage system which made the bureaucracy more responsive to the people by making the bureaucracy responsive to the party in power."[14] Jackson believed that responsiveness could be achieved because the people could hold the party accountable at the election polls.

It may be worthwhile to examine the activities of political bosses and machines in various cities to determine how responsive they were to the people. The boss was a dominant factor in the political system in American cities for almost three generations.[15]

When one views the outcomes of "the boss and machine" organization it is difficult to be judgmental. While the political machines can be held accountable for considerable corruption, they also, simultaneously, helped to assimilate new groups into American society and provided them with resources to move ahead. It has been suggested that "The parties frequently mismanaged urban growth on a grand scale, but they *did* manage urban growth at a time when other instrumentalities for governing the cities were inadequate."[16]

CIVIL SERVICE REFORM MOVEMENT

As discussed earlier, in order to comprehend discriminatory aspects of the merit system, it is necessary to examine the character of the civil service reform movement in the second half of the nineteenth century, which was established to undermine the patronage system. The reform movement focused its attack on the linkage between the public service and partisan politics.

The aftermath of the Civil War brought an extension of the spoils system, as well as the birth of the civil service reform movement. Excesses in the use of patronage coupled with a growing awareness of the defects of the spoils system provoked such eastern liberal reformers as George William Curtis and Thomas Jenckes as well as political independents such as Carl Schurz and William Dudley Foulke to a civil service reform movement that would replace the spoils system with the merit system. Their thesis was that government could not sacrifice quality and competence to favoritism.[17]

The primary focus of the reform movement was modification of the segment of the spoils system that delegated to local political bosses the authority to appoint local officials. The thrust of the reform was twofold: (1) to improve the efficiency of government, and (2) to remove the spoils system and thereby protect the republic.[18]

In his study of the civil service reform movement, Ari Hoogenboom refers to the reformers as "businessmen," but he is not referring to the masses of businessmen who flourished in this era. Rather, he is referring to those who inherited their business interests. The contrast is between established wealth and the *nouveau riche*.[19]

Politics and public service were controlled largely by the upper classes in the early years of the country. Robert Dahl, for example, in his discussion of power in New Haven, Connecticut, writes about political influence by the patrician class from approximately 1780 to 1840. In the period following 1840, however, the upper class gradually lost control of the political process and public service to the entreprenurial class, as well as to immigrant groups who found some degree of political power through local political machines. It is against this backdrop of a loss of political power that the reform movement must be viewed.[20]

Studies have indicated that the leaders of the various state civil service reform organizations were "overwhelmingly Protestant; they belonged to churches not only noted for an intellectual approach but for social position as well."[21] Hoogenboom points out that these state organizations contained a great number of the entrepreneurial group as members (to promote the goal of business efficiency in government), but these men were not the leaders in the movement.

The reformers were displaced patricians trying to regain political power from the *nouveau riche* and the immigrant-supported machines.[22] An hypothesis emerging from a body of literature on civil service reform suggests that the source of power for reform in urban government came from the upper class and not, as frequently believed, the lower or middle classes. What is significant is the attempt by these businessmen and professionals to shift the locus of power from a decentralized ward system, representative in municipal affairs of lower- and middle-class interests, to a more expansive scope of city affairs in which their own conception of public policy could dominate.[23]

The first result of national reform agitation was the Jenckes bill passed in the Ulysses S. Grant administration. President Grant was supportive of civil service reform; he supported a civil service reform bill and signed the Civil Service Act of 1871. Congress effectively opposed the system by denying funding after 1873. Despite the short existence of the Civil Service Commission created under Grant, many of the merit principles formulated by that body form the basis for the current civil service system.[24]

The opposition to civil service was based primarily on the fear of the politicians that the loss of patronage would erode their political base. The stated motive of the group, however, was different; they suggested in public that the system was unworkable, expensive, and perhaps even unconstitutional.

After the Civil Service Commission was curtailed and Grant's active support waned, the reform movement channeled its efforts into the nomination and election of candidates favorable to civil service reform. Generally, the reformers found that their candidates came out more strongly for civil service reform in their campaigns than they did in office. The reformers, however, continued their efforts.

The assassination of James Garfield by a frustrated seeker of patronage employment mobilized both the reformers and the general public. The reform press hit home with the idea that Garfield's assassination was simply a result of the spoils system. This provided a final impetus for the passage of the Pendleton Civil Service Act of 1883.[25] The Pendleton Act marked the initiation of a merit system for the United States public service. It was characterized as a recruitment system based on competitive examinations, relative security of tenure, and political neutrality.[26] It implied that these procedures would guarantee recruitment on the basis of objective measures of competence. It also assumed that political commitments would be eliminated as a *sine qua non* for employment.

If one analyzes the goals of the reformers, as discussed earlier, against their achievements, their success becomes evident. The introduction of merit principles added some measure of business efficiency as well as removing the spoils. They also succeeded to a small extent in restoring the social status of the civil service by recruiting individuals with a higher social status than those hired under the patronage system.[27] Civil service reform did not return the patrician to power, but it did start to destroy the immigrant machines and the ability of the *nouveau riche* to buy political power.

MERIT SYSTEM

As previously indicated, the Pendleton Act of 1883 introduced the merit system into the federal public service. Those who support the merit system now seem to have lost track of its original goals regarding political neutrality and accessibility at all levels. The term "merit," used to describe the system that replaced the patronage system, may have assured its "acceptance and protection."[28] This study will attempt to analyze whether the original goals of the merit system have been attained.

The same movement seen on the national level for civil service reform was also prevalent in the states. In New York, a movement led by the Republican Theodore Roosevelt was eventually successful despite opposition from New York Democrats who were in power. The bill passed in 1883 in New York was similar to the Pendleton Act.[29] It established a board of three commissioners to supervise a system of competitive examinations for appointments. Another aspect of the bill was that cities with populations exceeding 50,000 persons could apply civil service regulations to their cities if they desired (the bill did not apply to smaller cities).

Civil service reform was adopted in Massachusetts in 1884 as well.[30] The Massachusetts Civil Service Reform League also wrote a bill based on the Pendleton and New York acts. Its distinctive feature was that rules were to be drawn up by the state civil service commission instead of the city commissions as in New York.[31]

The principle of social equity was necessarily abandoned under the merit system. Under the patronage system, recruitment procedures allowed for a cross-section of the population to enter public service without regard to level of education achieved. Only those who had achieved a certain level of education were eligible for jobs under the merit system. The goals of merit principles cannot be realized if "a substantial part of the population is effectively denied the opportunity and/or the motivation to compete on an equal basis through culture and educational impoverishment."[32]

The 1980 Bureau of the Census figures provide information on those persons twenty-five years old and older who are high school graduates. Of those individuals in this age group in the whole population in the United States, 66.3 percent have completed high school. Broken down by race or ethnic groups, 68.7 percent of the whites, 50.6 percent of the blacks, and 43.3 percent of the individuals of Spanish origin have completed high school. Data for New York State indicate that 68.9 percent of the whites, 56.8 percent of the blacks, and 37.4 percent of the individuals of Spanish origin in this age group graduated from high school. In the New York metropolitan area 68 percent of the whites, 56.3 percent of the blacks, and 35.4 percent of the individuals of Spanish origin twenty-five years and older were high school graduates. If high school graduation is a minimum qualification for entrance into the merit system, fewer blacks and persons of Spanish origin than whites are eligible for these jobs.[33]

The status of immigrant groups in American society has denied them access to many jobs they would have been recruited for under the patronage system. As noted earlier, what emerged was a theory and practice of meritocracy which assumed that the best candidates were those who were most literate and most educated.[34]

In his work *Public Personnel Administration*, O. Glenn Stahl has attributed the growth of professionalization and competence in government employment to the merit system.[35] Personnel departments and civil service commissions on state and local levels established to ensure "neutral competence" in merit systems

soon shared their influence in this area with growing professional organizations and municipal employee unions. We have
seen a shift in formal and informal personnel control from the
designated personnel authorities to professional groups.[36]
Professional groups in turn have become strong defenders of a
civil service system that serves their interests as professionals.

The conflict between personnel theory and practice outlined
presents some serious implications for American politics. One
must question whether earlier commitment to a democratic public service has been hindered by the growth of a merit civil service
enhanced by professionalization and unionization whose objectives focus on "the welfare and advancement of their members."[37]

Considering some of the questions raised concerning equity
under the merit system it may be worthwhile focusing on the
notion of whether or not quality and social equity are compatible.

COMPATIBILITY OF QUALITY AND SOCIAL EQUITY

Michael Young's interesting book *The Rise of the Meritocracy
1870–2033: An Essay on Education and Equality* (1958) traces the
hypothetical history of English society and the transformation
of a patronage system to a merit civil service where achievement
became the standard for advancement. The only problem was
that the education system was not run on the same civil service
principle. Educational opportunity was a factor of class rather
than ability. Thus:

Some children of an ability which should have qualified them as assistant secretaries were forced to leave school at fifteen and become
postmen. Assistant secretaries delivering letters!—it is almost incredi-
ble. Other children with poor ability but rich connexions, pressed
through Eton and Balliol, eventually found themselves in mature years
as high officers in the Foreign Service.[38]

At the conclusion of the book, the year 2034, the Populists had
revolted. They had fostered a movement whose demands were
equality for all, and a classless society. Opportunity would no
longer be based on an IQ measure and each person would de-

velop on her/his own.[39] The British model offers a convenient basis for comparison with the merit system in the United States.

This study will attempt to examine the concepts of "social equity" and "neutral competence" as they relate to the civil service system. Using Michael Young's example, "social equity" is defined here as the ability of each person to have equal opportunity and develop on her/his own regardless of class. The concept of "neutral competence" would be based on an open competitive examination system as well as equal access to education.

During the period from 1940 to 1960, the merit system was so basic in the minds of most citizens, politicians, and academicians that the main consideration by these groups was how to strengthen it and broaden its scope. In the 1960s, however, the merit system came under strong attack. The attack was related to the beliefs that had been embraced during the prior generation. The proponents of the merit system claimed that the employees hired through the merit system were representative of the population that they served, and that the openness of the system provided the opportunity for persons in the lower echelons of society to use the civil service as a route to upward mobility, while at the same time representing the population which they served.[40]

On examination of the system, it was discovered that not all of the claims were true. It appeared that the merit system was not representative of all levels of society. Whether such an outcome was deliberate or the result of excluding people who were inadequately prepared to perform within the government, a demand arose among those groups denied access to the system. These groups pressed for a more representative civil service and created a movement for equal employment opportunity and affirmative action.[41]

In calling for social equity for public servants, public administration must balance that policy against the value premise of neutral competence in the public service. In examining efforts to achieve social equity in civil service, one must look at the development of the system, and the various programs designed for that purpose. Many of these programs were created to recruit minority groups for the public service. They emerged in response to charges of discrimination in the regular civil service system. Data indicated that, although the civil service served as an important source of minority employment as compared to the private sector, the number of minority people in such systems was minimal.[42]

In their study, Samuel Bowles and Herbert Gintis discussed the relationship between the education system and social equity. They concluded that:

The educational system legitimates economic inequality by providing an open, objective, and ostensibly meritocratic mechanism for assigning individuals to unequal economic positions. The educational system fosters and reinforces the belief that economic success depends essentially on the possession of technical and cognitive skills—skills which it is organized to provide in an efficient, equitable, and unbiased manner on the basis of meritocratic principle.

Of course, the use of the educational system to legitimize inequality is not without its own problems. Ideologies and structures which serve to hide and preserve one form of injustice often provide the basis of an assault on another. The ideology of equal educational opportunity and meritocracy is precisely such a contradictory mechanism.[43]

And yet, the values of meritocracy remain strong despite the pressure for remedial action and other egalitarian measures. A recent study of public administrators, drawn from all regions of the country and at all levels of government, concluded that "the overwhelming majority of officials still cling to the traditional merit precept: that government ought to hire the most competent individuals available."[44] This highlights the tension between patronage systems and merit systems concepts. It has been suggested that while patronage systems seek to "maximize bureaucratic responsiveness, . . . merit systems seek to maximize bureaucratic competence" by reliance on tests and other criteria.[45]

One should consider that the concept of social equity as it relates to the merit system has broad implications for democracy. In their study of political participation in America, Sidney Verba and Norman H. Nie agree that public policy emanating from citizen participation is preferable to a "more despotic policy." Participation is valuable because it can result in a more responsive and accountable government. In addition, if the democratic value of citizen participation is offered equal access to all citizens, it can be a resource to enhance social equity.[46]

Peter Bachrach continues this argument in his book *The Theory of Democratic Elitism*. Bachrach states:

> The crucial issue of democracy is not the composition of the elite— for the man on the bottom it makes little difference whether the command emanates from an elite of the rich and the wellborn or from an elite of workers and farmers. Instead the issue is whether democracy can diffuse power sufficiently throughout society to inculcate among people of all walks of life a justifiable feeling that they have the power to participate in decisions which affect themselves and the common life of the community, especially the immediate community in which they work and spend most of their waking hours and energy.[47]

Thus, one can also argue that social equity as it relates to the bureaucracy can also lead to more responsive government.

It has been argued that the concepts of merit and equity are indeed compatible. Harry Kranz frames the question, "Can we have both a 'representative bureaucracy' in which minorities and women are equitably distributed, and a 'merit system' of selecting government employees?" The conflict between "merit" and "equity," it is suggested, is an outgrowth of two myths which have arisen around the goals of the bureaucracy and the role of the merit system in choosing a highly competent government workforce.[48]

Kranz argues that a "representative bureaucracy" is beneficial for political, economic, and social reasons. He also suggests that it is a myth that most civil service employees are chosen largely on the basis of merit, "usually evidenced by fair written tests, and that the 'best and the brightest' survive this scientific process to be appointed to federal, state, and local jobs."[49] Even in Thomas Jefferson's appointment days intellect was not necessarily considered the most important element of merit qualities. Qualities of "the heart, or honesty, integrity, loyalty, and patriotism" were considered more important.[50]

In arguing for the compatibility of merit and equity one can suggest that selection procedures designed to predict on-the-job performance of a person would be compatible with the original goals of the civil service system. However, by eliminating "discriminatory selection devices and criteria and substituting methods designed to achieve social equity for under-represented minorities and women, we will be achieving a truly meritorious public service—one by, as well as for, all the people."[51]

The conflict outlined, concerning the compatibility of "neutral competence" and "social equity," presents some serious implications for administrative and personnel theory and practice. If public administrators are to reconcile the differences between these two concepts it will be necessary to attack aspects of the present merit system that eliminate particular groups from having access to the system. Further, unless class as a factor in educational opportunity is discarded, it will be difficult to reconcile the two concepts.

RAWLS ON SOCIAL JUSTICE

In order to better understand some of the discriminatory aspects of municipal civil service systems, it may be useful to examine the concept of social justice offered by John Rawls. The concept, however, is not simple.[52] A critique of Rawls' work by one political scientist states that:

Inequality is the most general of social facts. . . . It is, moreover, difficult to imagine men and women so docile as not to invest these differences with coherent social value and thus to discover the inequalities which separate them from one another. But when if ever are these inequalities legitimate? On what argument may life's winners excuse themselves to those who are left behind? On which terms may the deprived rightly overturn privilege?[53]

Douglas Rae suggests that these are the main practical questions of social justice.

John Rawls defines justice this way: "A conception of social justice, then, is to be regarded as providing in the first instance a standard whereby the distributive aspects of the basic structure of society are to be assessed."[54]

Refining the concept further, for Rawls, justice is fairness, and the foundation of fairness rests initially on two principles:

First Principle

Each person is to have an equal right to the most extensive total system of equal basic liberties compatible with a similar system of liberty for all.

Second Principle

Social and economic inequalities are to be arranged so that they are both:
   a. to the greatest benefit of the least advantaged . . . , and
   b. attached to offices and positions open to all under conditions of fair equality of opportunity.[55]

In a study of discrimination of women in the workforce, Mary Lepper applies Rawls' concept to the problem. She suggests that Rawls argues that it will be necessary to eliminate the causes of social inequity if society is unjust. A just society, however, only requires monitoring. Our society does not meet Rawls' second principle of what constitutes justice. Thus, we face an unjust society and look to remedial justice as a means to eliminate those social inequities.[56] While inequities, however, are thought to be unfair, there are those who view attempts at remedying these social ills as an intrusion.[57]

Lepper uses affirmative action as an example of a mechanism to "overcome the existing allocations of benefits in a society whereby some have been disadvantaged as a result of 'natural chance or the contingency of social circumstances.' "[58]

This argument can be applied to the premise of this study that municipal civil service systems and the principle of meritocracy underlying that system have contributed to and maintained a system of social inequity. If one follows Rawls' concept, then one could argue that society is obligated to dismantle the barriers which have contributed to and maintained social inequity in the civil service.

BANFIELD AND WILSON: A CLASS POSITION

Edward C. Banfield and James Q. Wilson suggest that, although all of the goals of the municipal reformers have not been met, "city government is vastly, more honest, efficient, and

democratic than it was a generation or two ago." They attribute
these alleged improvements to "the steady diffusion in our culture of the political ideal of the Anglo-Saxon Protestant middle-
class political ethos."[59] This book will examine their premise
since the challenge to the civil service system as lacking in competence and equity has intensified in the current era.

In *City Politics*, Banfield and Wilson develop a theory to explain
aspects of American municipal politics. Their theory of "public
regardingness" and "private regardingness" states that much of
what Americans think about politics can be categorized under
one or the other aspect of the theory and "that the prevalence
of one ethos over the other influences the style, structure, and
outcome of local politics."[60] Banfield and Wilson hypothesize
that the formation of political systems and public policy can be
attributed to these two ethics in the population.

In an article which examines some of the premises of the
Banfield and Wilson theory, Raymond Wolfinger and John Field
suggest that Banfield and Wilson "take their cue" from Richard
Hofstadter's *The Age of Reform* in developing their theory. Hofstadter contrasts native and immigrant political values in the
early twentieth century. He suggests that native political values,
based upon Yankee-Protestant traditions and middle-class life,
assumed that political life was to be run with little citizen involvement and separate from personal needs. In contrast, the
urban machine was based upon the values of the European
backgrounds of the immigrants, with their familiarity with authority, loyalty, and the basic needs which were an outgrowth
of migration.[61]

Banfield and Wilson expand on this theory in their interpre-
tation of municipal politics. They note that issues arise out of
the more lasting divisions in the society which they call cleavages. These cleavages—"between the haves and have-nots, the
suburbanites and the central city, the natives and the immigrants, and the major political parties"—tend to "coalesce into
two opposed patterns." They are described as follows:

> These patterns reflect two conceptions of the public interest that are
> widely held. The first, which derives from the middle-class ethos, favors
> what the municipal reform movement has always defined as "good

government"—namely efficiency, impartiality, honesty, planning, strong executives, no favoritism, model legal codes, and strict enforcement of laws against gambling and vice. The other conception of the public interest (one never explicitly formulated as such, but one all the same) derives from the "immigrant ethos." This is the conception of those people who identify with the ward or neighborhood rather than the city "as a whole," who look to politicians for "help" and "favors," who regard gambling and vice as, at worst, necessary evils, and who are far less interested in the efficiency, impartiality, and honesty of local government than in its readiness to confer material benefits of one sort or another upon them.[62]

In a later article, Banfield and Wilson refine their argument. The "middle-class" Anglo-Saxon Protestants they wrote about in *City Politics*, they claim, would have been better described as "upper-class" or "upper-middle-class." They use the term "private-regarding," in *City Politics*, in reference to immigrant and working-class ethos, and consider that:

Possibly such voters take into account public needs but define the public differently than do upper-class Anglo-Saxons, thinking of it as their immediate neighborhood or their own racial, ethnic, or occupational group, rather than as the "community as a whole."[63]

What is significant is that the Banfield and Wilson theory provides a model in which the input of the "Anglo-Saxon Protestant middle-class political ethos" in the municipal reform movement results in positive feedback. They do not account for the fact that working class and immigrant groups were a major part of the spoils system and patronage system; the reform movement prompted the destruction of the political machines and denied these working class and immigrant groups access to political power. It should also be noted that the reformers modeled the United States civil service system after the upper-class-oriented civil service of Great Britain.

It is with this backdrop in mind that this study will focus on the challenges to a civil service system that is rooted in an upper-class bias.

CREDENTIALLING AS A MAJOR ROUTE TO MERITOCRACY

The *Random House Dictionary*[64] defines *meritocracy* as "a class of persons making their way on their own ability and talent rather than because of class privileges." The *merit system* in the United States is defined as "a system or practice in which persons are hired or promoted on the basis of ability rather than patronage." The traditional definition of merit is changing for a segment of the public service and is increasingly being measured by standards set by professionals.

A study of job classifications in Philadelphia noted that:

The overqualification of personnel is hardly a phenomenon unique to government. Because the protection of the inept is a pervasive feature of all societies, higher standards are usually set for obtaining a craft or white collar job than for performance. The result is that a high level or formal education is often necessary for jobs that any average eighth-grader could learn to perform rather quickly.[65]

The Philadelphia study presents evidence supporting the notion that professional groups frequently demand that standards for public service positions as described in job specifications be unreasonably high. These requisites can range, for example, from rigid educational or experience requirements to examinations.[66]

Unfortunately, there are greater political implications related to the concept of "social equity" for overcredentialling. At a time when all levels of government claim to be attempting to recruit minorities into public service it seems contradictory to impose false credentialling. Overcredentialling is significant because of the implication of those holding such government jobs also governing the community. There is a relationship between the index of political power and the numbers of respective groups in the public service.[67]

Further, evidence indicates that often these credentialling restrictions, often requirements for even sitting for an examination, have little or no relation to job performance. In fact, Ivar Berg suggests that there is:

more evidence to support the proposition that educational credentials *as such* have relatively little bearing on performance; the extent to which public services function well is apparently related to other factors, including the managerial skills of those in responsible and accountable positions.[68]

Berg also observes that educational credentials have become the new property in America, reinforcing a class barrier.[69] Under these conditions social equity goals may be in direct conflict with merit requirements.

Daniel Bell, for one, views a "meritocratic society as a 'credentials society' in which the certification of achievement— through the college degree, the professional examination, the license—becomes a condition of higher employment."[70] Thus, education is seen as the major network or route to meritocracy. All education institutions, however, are not viewed equally. Most large law firms, for example, hire mainly from Ivy League colleges. And, in fact, exclusionary rules and nepotism often determine who succeeds.

The demands by minority groups, women, and the hard-core unemployed for equal educational opportunity, however, are related to the need for credentials. Even Bell admits that this is the reasoning behind the demands for "open admissions" to universities, and the land-grant college acts. However, as one advocate of open admissions notes:

As long as open admissions remains limited to a few institutions, it poses no threat to the meritocracy. Recruitment into the elite will be based not on *whether* one went to college, but on *where* one went to college. Universal open admissions, however, would destroy the close articulation between the meritocracy and the system of higher education; further, by the very act of abolishing hierarchy in admissions, it would cast doubt on hierarchy in the larger society.[71]

If open admissions became a policy for all universities it could provide a thrust for reconciling the concepts of "social equity" and "neutral competence."

There have been various attempts at reconciling the conflict of "social equity" with the merit system. This study will examine some of these efforts, including affirmative action programs, litigation and legislation aimed at eliminating discriminatory aspects of civil service systems, and public employment programs. It will evaluate the success of these efforts against the continuing concern with maintaining a merit system which can be an instrument of exclusion.

NOTES

1. Edward C. Banfield and James Q. Wilson, *City Politics* (New York: Vintage Books, 1963), p. 207.

2. Samuel P. Hays, "The Politics of Reform in Municipal Government in the Progressive Era," in *Social Change and Urban Politics: Readings*, ed. Daniel N. Gordon (Englewood Cliffs, N.J.: Prentice-Hall, 1973), p. 108.

3. Frank J. Thompson, "Meritocracy, Equality and Employment: Commitment to Minority Hiring Among Public Officials," paper presented at the 1976 Annual Meeting of the American Political Science Association, Chicago, 2–5 September 1976, p. 1.

4. Paul P. Van Riper, *History of the United States Civil Service* (Evanston, Ill.: Row, Peterson and Company, 1958).

5. Ibid., p. 8.

6. Ari Hoogenboom, *Outlawing the Spoils: A History of the Civil Service Reform Movement 1865–1883* (Urbana, Ill.: University of Illinois Press, 1961), p. 4.

7. Harold F. Gortner, *Administration in the Public Sector* (New York: John Wiley & Sons, 1977), p. 269.

8. Arthur M. Schlesinger, Jr., *The Age of Jackson* (Boston: Little, Brown and Company, 1945), p. 47.

9. Frederick C. Mosher, *Democracy and the Public Service* (New York: Oxford University Press, 1968), p. 63.

10. Bertram M. Gross and Jeffrey F. Kraus, "The Political Machine Is Alive and Well," *Social Policy* 12 (Winter 1982): 38.

11. David L. Martin, *Running City Hall: Municipal Administration in America* (University, Ala.: The University of Alabama Press, 1982), p. 3.

12. Ann Cook, Marilyn Gittell, and Herb Mack, eds., *City Life, 1865–1900: Views of Urban America* (New York: Praeger Publishers, 1973), p. 177. See also Charles N. Glaab and A. Theodore Brown, *A History of Urban America* (New York: The Macmillan Company, 1967).

13. Gross and Kraus, "The Political Machine Is Alive and Well," p. 38.

14. Kenneth M. Meier, "Ode to Patronage: A Critical Analysis of

Two Recent Supreme Court Decisions," *Public Administration Review* 41 (September/October 1981): 558.

15. Glaab and Brown, *A History of Urban America*, p. 202. For studies of bosses in American cities see J. T. Salter, *Boss Rule: Portraits in City Politics* (New York: McGraw-Hill Book Company, 1935); Warren Moscow, *The Last of the Big-Time Bosses: The Life and Times of Carmine DeSapio and the Rise and Fall of Tammany Hall* (New York: Stein and Day, 1971); and William Riordan, *Plunkitt of Tammany Hall* (New York: E. P. Dutton & Company, 1963). For a discussion of the continuance of bossism in Jersey City following the defeat of Frank Hague see William Lemmey, "Bossism in Jersey City: The Kenny Years, 1949–1972" (Ph.D diss., City University of New York, 1979).

16. Fred I. Greenstein, "The Changing Pattern of Urban Party Politics," *The Annals of the American Academy of Political and Social Science* 353 (May 1964): 7.

17. Hoogenboom, *Outlawing the Spoils*; for a description of the position of some of these reformers see The National Civil-Service Reform League, *Proceedings of the Annual Meeting Held at Washington, D.C., December 12 and 13, 1895. With the Address of the President, Hon. Carl Schurz, and Other Matters* (New York: National Civil-Service Reform League, 1895); and William Dudley Foulke, *Fighting the Spoilsmen* (New York: The Knickerbocker Press, 1919), p. 6; for a discussion of the work of the National Civil Service Reform League and its contributions to the civil service reform movement in the United States see Frank Mann Stewart, *The National Civil Service League: History, Activities, and Problems* (Austin, Texas: The University of Texas, 1929).

18. Hoogenboom, *Outlawing the Spoils*.

19. Ibid., pp. 179–197.

20. Robert A. Dahl, *Who Governs? Democracy and Power in an American City* (New Haven: Yale University Press, 1961), pp. 11–31.

21. Hoogenboom, *Outlawing the Spoils*, pp. 179–197.

22. Ibid., p. 196.

23. Hays, "The Politics of Reform in Municipal Government," pp. 113–118.

24. Gortner, *Administration in the Public Sector*, pp. 270–271.

25. Ibid., p. 271. See also John M. Dobson, *Politics in the Gilded Age: A New Perspective on Reform* (New York: Praeger Publishers, 1972).

26. Van Riper, *History of the United States Civil Service*, p. 100.

27. Ari Hoogenboom, "Outlawing the Spoils" (Ph.D. diss., Columbia University, 1957), p. 433.

28. Marilyn Gittell, "Putting Merit Back in the Merit System," *Social Policy* 3 (September/October 1972): 20.

29. Robert D. Lee, Jr., *Public Personnel Systems* (Baltimore: University Park Press, 1979), p. 22.

30. Ibid.; for a review of civil service reform in Massachusetts see George C. S. Benson, *The Administration of the Civil Service in Massachusetts: With Special Reference to State Control of City Civil Service* (Cambridge, Mass.: Harvard University Press, 1935), pp. 1–19.

31. Hoogenboom, *Outlawing the Spoils*, pp. 257–258. It is interesting to note that Dobson in *Politics in the Gilded Age*, p. 34, states that, "with a few noteworthy exceptions, such as the creation of a merit civil service system, the federal government tended to follow rather than lead the states in political innovation."

32. Mosher, *Democracy and the Public Service*.

33. U.S. Department of Commerce, Bureau of the Census, *1980 Census of Population and Housing. Provisional Estimates of Social, Economic, and Housing Characteristics* (Washington, D.C.: U.S. Government Printing Office, March 1982).

34. Van Riper, *History of the United States Civil Service*.

35. O. Glenn Stahl, *Public Personnel Administration* (New York: Harper & Row, 1971), pp. 29–41.

36. Gittell, "Putting Merit Back in the Merit System," p. 20.

37. Mosher, *Democracy and the Public Service*, pp. 2, 209.

38. Michael Young, *The Rise of the Meritocracy 1870–2033: An Essay on Education and Equality* (Middlesex, England: Penguin Books, 1961), p. 20.

39. Young, *The Rise of the Meritocracy*.

40. Gortner, *Administration in the Public Sector*, p. 273.

41. Ibid.

42. Don Hellriegel and Larry Short, "Equal Employment Opportunity in the Federal Government: A Comparative Analysis," *Public Administration Review* 32 (November/December 1972): 851–857.

43. Samuel Bowles and Herbert Gintis, *Schooling in Capitalist America: Educational Reform and the Contradictions of Economic Life* (New York: Basic Books, 1976), p. 103.

44. Thompson, "Meritocracy, Equality and Employment," p. 15.

45. Meier, "Ode to Patronage," p. 559.

46. Sidney Verba and Norman H. Nie, *Participation in America: Political Democracy and Social Equality* (New York: Harper & Row, 1972), pp. 334–335.

47. Peter Bachrach, *The Theory of Democratic Elitism: A Critique* (Boston: Little, Brown and Company, 1967), p. 92.

48. Harry Kranz, "Are Merit and Equity Compatible?" *Public Administration Review* 34 (September/October 1974): 434.

49. Ibid., p. 436.

50. For a discussion of appointments in the early days of the Republic, see Sidney H. Aronson, *Status and Kinship in the Higher Civil Service: Standards of Selection in the Administrations of John Adams, Thomas Jefferson, and Andrew Jackson* (Cambridge, Mass.: Harvard University Press, 1964), p. 16.

51. Kranz, "Are Merit and Equity Compatible?" p. 439.

52. For extensive critiques of John Rawls', *A Theory of Justice*, see "Justice: A Spectrum of Responses to John Rawls's Theory," *The American Political Science Review* 69 (June 1975): 588–674; and Robert Paul Wolff, *Understanding Rawls: A Reconstruction and Critique of "A Theory of Justice"* (Princeton, N.J.: Princeton University Press, 1977).

53. Douglas Rae, "Maximin Justice and an Alternative Principle of General Advantage," *The American Political Science Review* 69 (June 1975): 630.

54. John Rawls, *A Theory of Justice* (Cambridge, Mass.: The Belknap Press of Harvard University Press, 1971), p. 9.

55. Ibid., p. 302.

56. Mary M. Lepper, "The Status of Women in the United States, 1976: Still Looking for Justice and Equity," *Public Administration Review* 36 (July/August 1976): 367.

57. Robert E. Lane, "Market Justice, Political Justice," *American Political Science Review* 80 (June 1986): 397.

58. Lepper, "The Status of Women in the United States, 1976," p. 367.

59. Banfield and Wilson, *City Politics*, pp. 149–150.

60. Raymond E. Wolfinger and John Osgood Field, "Political Ethos and the Structure of City Government," *The American Political Science Review* 60 (June 1966): 306.

61. Richard Hofstadter, *The Age of Reform* (New York: Knopf, 1955), pp. 8–9, quoted in Wolfinger and Field, "Political Ethos and the Structure of City Government," p. 46.

62. Banfield and Wilson, *City Politics*, p. 46.

63. James Q. Wilson and Edward C. Banfield, "Political Ethos Revisited," *The American Political Science Review* 65 (December 1971): 1048–1049.

64. *The Random House Dictionary of the English Language, College Edition* (New York: Random House, 1968), p. 837.

65. Jay M. Shafritz, *Position Classification: A Behavioral Analysis for the Public Service* (New York: Praeger Publishers, 1973), p. 26.

66. Ibid.

67. Ibid., p. 27.

68. Ivar Berg, *Education and Jobs: The Great Training Robbery* (Boston: Beacon Press, 1971), p. 175.

69. Ibid., p. 185.

70. Daniel Bell, "Meritocracy and Equality," *The Public Interest*, no. 29 (Fall 1972): 34.

71. Ibid., pp. 34–35.

The Impact of Current Practices and Procedures in Civil Service

2

The practices and procedures in municipal civil service systems have a significant impact on the ability of minorities and women to compete for jobs within civil service systems. Determining those who control public policy is critical to understanding the policy and in any effort to change that policy. This chapter will focus on the processes and the actors involved in civil service decision making. The major participants—personnel professionals, civil service commissions, professional organizations, and municipal unions—will all be examined in terms of their impact on this process. The role of the mayor as providing leadership for change in what seems to be a closed system will be evaluated. The effect of qualifications, examinations, and promotional requirements on "social equity" within the merit system will also be addressed.

As suggested earlier, the reform movement changed the mechanisms for organizing politics. A shift in the basic power structure of cities occurred, which moved the locus of power from ward constituencies to citywide authority. The power of ethnic and racial groups was therefore undermined.[1] A study of Los Angeles indicates that, as a result of governmental reforms, civil servants became a political force. The reform was characterized by a strong mayor, council, and appointed administrators. Moreover, because reform prompted candidates to emphasize the entire electorate in their campaigns, making publicity more important than familiarity with individual constituents, the change weakened the influence of local neighborhood associations and racial and ethnic groups, and increased the importance of metropolitan institutions.[2]

A study of the impact of municipal affirmative action programs on black representation in government employment concludes that reformed government structures created barriers to the expansion of black bureaucratic representation. In the past, city jobs have served as a resource of political power, and as a major route to mobility for Italians, Irish, and Jews. Blacks as the newcomers do not have the same accessibility to these positions. Blacks have attempted to enter the public service at a time when older immigrant groups have preempted these positions and access to the system is constrained by civil service provisions and collective bargaining.[3] Obviously, the extent to which inequality will continue to exist within bureaucracies is dependent upon the attitude of those personnel administrators responsible for recruiting and promoting individuals within civil service systems.[4] Administrators who are proponents of hiring minorities and women are, for example, less apt to promote increased credentials as requirements for positions.[5]

The study of urban public policy can help to explain the power relationships in cities. Evaluation of particular urban policies will indicate whether government responds to the requirements of poorer groups or more affluent special-interest groups in society.[6] Examination of current practices and procedures in municipal civil service systems should contribute to the understanding of power relationships in American cities.

DECISION MAKING IN THE CIVIL SERVICE AND INTEREST GROUP POLITICS

That interest groups are important participants in public policy development and implementation in the United States is well-documented.[7] Interest groups are also formed in response to the passage of particular legislation or the adoption of particular programs. Established interest groups direct their efforts and influence to mold the character of programs or policies. Bureaucracies responsible for implementing these policies often support the activities of interest groups that are compatible with their own views.[8] Bureaucrats also often have organizational interests apart from their individual political and social views. This study will review the relationship between the various actors in municipal civil service decision making to determine the orientation of civil service and personnel specialists as regards to the goal of social equity in civil service.

Robert Moses, a major figure in New York City and New York State bureaucracies, had an influential role in the civil service reform movement in New York City and the development of the city's merit system. In his doctoral thesis (later published as *The Civil Service of Great Britain*), Moses criticized the patronage system and advocated a merit system characterized by "open competition" as the basis of appointment and promotion in the public service. The merit he referred to was not in the public service but in the elitist education available to members of the upper class. Moses concluded that a civil service void of class differentiation is "one of mediocrity." In the last chapter of his thesis Moses argued that the United States should adopt the upper-class British system for its own civil service.[9]

What is significant in Robert Moses' orientation are the values held by reformers of that era. These were the values which shaped the merit system and civil service policy in American cities.

Civil Service Commissions, Personnel Departments, and Personnel Directors

The first civil service commissions emerged from the civil service reform movement. Their purpose was to free the public servant from political influence. These central personnel agencies were usually bipartisan in nature. Their major function was to ensure that individuals entered the public service only through "merit." In order to fulfill its obligations the typical commission was structured as a separate entity from the administrative hierarchy.[10]

Currently, there are two major types of public personnel organizations in use in cities, the independent civil service commission and the city personnel department. The civil service commission, typically, is comprised of three to five members, designated on a bipartisan or nonpartisan basis by a chief administrator or municipal governing council to serve part-time for long terms. The commission usually is responsible for the job classification plan, including establishing qualifications and preparing examinations. Commissions often hire a full-time chief examiner to implement the examination and hiring process. The commissioners also maintain responsibility for grievance and disciplinary procedures. In contrast, the role of the city personnel department is a staff function, headed by a personnel director who is generally appointed by and reports to the chief administrator. The two systems have been combined in some cities by having the personnel director also function as chief administrator to the civil service commission.[11]

A survey of the personnel systems of state and local governments, conducted by the National Civil Service League, concluded that the organization of the typical personnel system was headed by a civil service commission with a full-time personnel officer supervising the functions of a central personnel office.[12]

In 1972, the International City Management Association conducted a survey of cities and counties to determine the role of civil service commissions in their personnel systems. This survey confirms that the role and influence of commissions vary, with the scope of their responsibilities for most often limited to hearing appeals or validating personnel rules and regulations. Moreover, the survey suggests that "existing personnel rules and policies, union contracts, or political arrangements may limit the ability of chief executives to control and manage the personnel organization."[13]

It has been suggested that personnel managers can influence the shape of their agencies by utilizing "environmental variables (laws, expectations, and the relative power of competing groups)." The predictability of these variables is what makes it possible for them to be used effectively. These expectations contradict accepted assumptions about public personnel management.[14]

A study of female employment representation in twenty cities concludes that the attitudes of personnel directors influence the rate of female employment in municipal government regardless of community and organizational characteristics.[15] Thus, personnel directors are key participants in the decision making process in that they have the ability to influence employment outcomes.

From 1883 to 1954, New York City personnel policy consisted primarily of the protection of the basic principles of merit mandated by New York State civil service laws. This was accomplished by a Municipal Civil Service Commission whose duties included the establishment and maintenance of civil service rules and regulations (including appointment, selection, promotion, and appeals procedures). The function covered the administration of examinations and the certification of lists based upon the result of the examination, as well as the creation of a classification plan for city employees and the recruitment of potential city workers.[16] The duties of the commission involved only minimally the question of citywide personnel management. Its prime function was to maintain the merit principle rather than implementing the principles of effective personnel administration.

The lack of any broad personnel administration within the New York City civil service structure became a consistent criticism of city personnel activity during the early 1950s.[17] Criticisms of the personnel system were based upon the underlying theme that a sound personnel policy necessitated more than merely protection of the merit principles. It required, as well, a positive policy of personnel administration based upon proven principles of scientific management. The area in which reformers saw the greatest opportunity to use scientific management principles in the interests of personnel administration was the need to develop comprehensive classification and compensation schedules.[18]

On March 31, 1954, the city charter was amended and a Department of Personnel was established in New York City. This new personnel agency, located in the Office of the Mayor, represented the bridging of merit interests with those of scientific personnel management. The director of the Department of Personnel would serve at the pleasure of the mayor and, while holding that position, would also chair the Civil Service Commission.[19]

The significance of the personnel management reform movement of the early 1950s, culminating in the creation of the New York City Department of Personnel, lies primarily in what was not accomplished by these policy reforms. None of the reforms dealt with the question of how to open up the civil service system to allow for the broader representation of groups such as minorities and women in the city workforce.

The "efficiency-management" orientation of the 1950s reforms not only ignored the thrusts of group equity within the city workforce, it further institutionalized practices and priorities that worked against minority needs. This is most apparent in the Department of Personnel's relationship with agency professionals. Their orientation was to rely heavily on the judgments of the agency's entrenched professional groups in determining such matters as credential requirements, promotional ladders, and job functions.

Except for the surge of activity in the area of classification and compensation, the Department of Personnel functioned in a manner similar to that of its organizational predecessor. In-service training programs, new recruitment programs, exam analysis and evaluation were clearly not the priorities of the new department, as they were not the priorities of the Municipal Civil Service Commission. After all, if the professionals were satisfied with the quality of their personnel, why should the staff-oriented Department of Personnel worry? Thus, reform was restricted to the area of classification and compensation and other routine efforts in the interests of a "merit" system.

On March 31, 1958, Mayor Robert F. Wagner issued Executive Order 49, whose effects within ten years would result in the effective demise of the Career and Salary Plan (a system approved in 1959 by which civil servants would be grouped by title in order to set salaries and make other personnel decisions). The order permitted employees represented by unions to bargain collectively with city representatives in an effort to ensure, among other things, increased compensation. When an agreement was reached, the classification and compensation schedules would be automatically changed reflecting the agreement.[20] The use of collective bargaining by municipal employees as an instrument for salary advancement became increasingly popular over the next few years.[21]

With individual unions playing such a major role in the determination of employee salary levels and in fixing their relationship between salary and job function, the Career and Salary Plan rapidly became a personnel anachronism.[22] In 1967, Mayor John V. Lindsay issued a personnel order abolishing the Career and Salary Plan for all employees who were covered by collective bargaining agreements. In its place, the Mayor created an Alternate Career and Salary Plan which was not a plan at all, but merely a document allowing the mayor to issue personnel implementing orders, certifying salary scales agreed upon in collective bargaining negotiations.[23]

Reports concluded that the civil service system was "inadequate, outdated, rigid, and largely 'meritless.' "[24] In 1975, a report was prepared for the State Charter Revision Commission concerning personnel reforms for New York City. The commission recommended that the New York City Charter should delegate substantial personnel responsibilities to city agencies, develop a management service to strengthen the city's middle-management staff, and restructure the Civil Service Commission "to make it an affirmative force in personnel management."[25]

While the Civil Service Commission has served as an alternate appeals route for employees, it is noteworthy that it was intended to be the watchdog of the city's personnel system. With the personnel director chairing the commission, it was unrealistic for the commission to review the policies and decisions of the Personnel Department.[26]

In November 1975, the voters approved revisions to the New York City Charter effective January 1, 1977. These revisions included changes in the city's personnel system. Following are some of these changes, which comprise the current system:

1. The Civil Service Commission was to be distinct from the personnel director, and the personnel director was to assume the administrative and rule-making authority of the Civil Service Commission.[27]

2. The Civil Service Commission would have the power to hear and determine appeals by persons aggrieved by any action of the per-

sonnel director, and it would have responsibility for conducting reviews of the personnel administration in the city.[28]

3. Agencies were to be given enhanced responsibility for personnel management functions.[29]

It is worthwhile noting that in recent years various cities saw the same problems that the reformers at the turn of the century observed. Both sets of reformers believed that the civil service system was unable to hire the most competent people available for positions. The turn-of-the century reformers saw patronage and favoritism as the culprit. More recent reformers view the system, which was originally designed to promote "merit and fitness," and protection from external influences, as being unresponsive to society's changing needs. This neo-reform movement cites the inability of municipal civil service systems to hire and promote minorities and women in civil service jobs in proportion to their representation in the population as a result of inflexible civil service systems, especially examination and promotion procedures and entrance qualifications.

Philadelphia commissioned a study in 1981 to review its civil service system. The panel preparing the report identified several weaknesses in Philadelphia's civil service system which have contributed to a loss of the positive side of merit, that is, having the most competent people available. Weaknesses include: (1) time lags of four to six months or more to fill vacancies due to an overloaded examination process; (2) an ineffective performance appraisal system; (3) an ineffective reward system to recognize contributions to the delivery of city services; (4) affirmative action procedures that lack focus and a systematic approach (minorities tend to be employed in paraprofessional and service maintenance jobs); and (5) training and development activities inadequate to meet broad needs.[30]

Charter revisions in Philadelphia were recommended by the panel to include appointment of the personnel director by the mayor to be accompanied by cabinet-level status. The emphasis of the personnel director's function was to be shifted away from technical activities toward policy-oriented personnel management compatible with merit principles.[31] In addition, the panel proposed a series of actions which would clarify the roles between the Personnel Department and the Civil Service Commission. Such actions would emphasize the "watchdog" and evaluation role of the Commission, particularly with regard to protecting merit principles.[32]

The creation of a more "professionalized" public service and the mechanism of public employee collective bargaining were more or less indirect offshoots of the change in personnel orientation from merit maintainers to personnel managers. The former occurred as a result of an implicit recognition of the value of the professional in the public service, this assumption totally consistent with management principles such as the "one best way to do a job" and the determination of position based on objective qualifications. Also important in this process was the classical conception of the department of personnel as a staff arm to agency interests. Collective bargaining was a reaction against another classical scientific management principle: that in the public service, it is necessary for the welfare of the city that the needs of employees must be objectively determined solely by the employer. Both offshoots have worked against the interests of an open personnel system. It is important, however, to recognize that besides protecting the interests of professionalism and strong subprofessional unions, the personnel department is also directly protecting the tools of scientific management itself. These tools are at the very heart of a personnel management system, and they are often used against the interests of an open civil service system.

This attitude is confirmed in an interview the author conducted with the former personnel director of a large city, who emphasized businesslike efficiency as an overriding concern in government operations. He would not likely accept any level of inefficiency in the name of providing more jobs. This emphasis on efficiency seems, in part, to be the basis for his rejection of on-the-job training programs. The personnel director characterized the personnel department as being responsible merely for implementing policy established by agencies and by collective bargaining. He minimized the policy implications of the department's responsibilities for administering the examination system. The director believed in the ability of the examination system to obtain qualified individuals; he implied that he would not support reducing qualifications in order to recruit the unskilled and unemployed. This attitude reflects his own progress through the civil service system. He was employed by the civil service system for more than 40 years, beginning in an entry-level position, moving through the ranks by passing seven promotional examinations, and culminating in the personnel director position. He clearly believes in the "bootstrap" theory, that the same route he followed up the career ladder is open to all entrants into the civil service system.[33]

Professional Organizations

Professional bureaucrats have been successful at amassing bureaucratic power. They have attained respect in American society not only for their reputed competence and expertise, but also because they contrast well with those who gain position as a result of patronage. Professional bureaucrats have succeeded in propelling the myth that they are neutral in policy issues and merely represent political officials in their actions.[34] Because professionals are viewed with deference in our society, they are permitted to act authoritatively on a broad range of political and social issues. Thus, it has been suggested, "While civil servants are not highly regarded by society, those civil servants who are also professionals have been able to combine the two factors to their advantage."[35]

Although John Stuart Mill focuses on the need for professionalism in the civil service, when he addresses the role of bureaucracy in a democracy he recognizes the need to maintain a balance.[36] When the effects of bureaucracy begin to overshadow the important value of participation, Mill reasserts the importance of participation and calls for a balance between participation and competence.[37]

Frederick Mosher is concerned that the emergence of professionals in public employment has revolutionized the principles and policies in government. These principles and policies are often antithetical to the basic tenets of civil service reform in America: "equal opportunity to apply and compete for jobs; competitive examinations for selection and (sometimes) promotion; equal pay for equal work; neutral and objective direction and control of the personnel system."[38]

The common belief of the 1950s reformers was that efficient personnel management meant, to a large extent, discovering from the "experts" what the "objective" job qualifications and functions were, and then institutionalizing these discoveries in a uniform, consistent personnel system.[39]

Professional bureaucracies had achieved status as contestants in the city's political system by organizing. Their organizations are plentiful. Some of them have large memberships, while others maintain influence in important aspects of the political process.[40]

Dependence on the "professional" worked directly against the interests of an open civil service system because professionals, in order to maintain and enhance their financial and social status, favored a closed personnel system. By restricting entrance in the civil service only to those who met their own definition of a qualified applicant, the professionals were legitimizing their role as possessor of a unique and socially beneficial skill, thereby enhancing their own social and economic worth. They were also helping to ensure the perpetuation of their own occupational value structures and ideologies by admitting into the profession only those whose training, background, skills, and knowledge were similar to their own and hence professionally acceptable. This pattern has been in existence in the private sector for more than a hundred years. Professions developed their own standards of requirements, and then turned to state law and constitution to enforce these standards, thereafter controlling the profession.[41]

The repercussions of this notion of standards determined by "professionals" is particularly meaningful in relation to questions of service. When the ideologies and value structures perpetuated by the professional recruitment process run counter to the interests of the communities being served by these professionals, unsatisfactory service results. Although the potential conflict of professional interest versus community interest is always present, it is most acute when the communities in question are severely underrepresented in the professional ranks. In such cases, there is much less incentive on the part of the organization to adjust their services to fit the needs of the community and yet, ironically, more need for it to do so. Often, the organization will protect itself in the face of community resentment by blaming service failure, not on the inadequacy of the organization, but on the inadequacy of the members of the community itself. In the 1960s, however, in many large American cities, many of the accepted notions of qualifications and professional behavior by teachers, lawyers, and doctors came under attack by the poor.[42]

Municipal Unions

The era of collective bargaining has brought about a fundamental change in the philosophy of personnel departments in cities where municipal unions are participants in the personnel policy processes. Before the existence of collective bargaining, the influence of employee needs and wants on personnel department activities was directly related to the degree of professionalism involved in the work activity. The greater the recognized professionalism of the tasks, the less interference by the personnel department in setting standards and job descriptions. So great was the personnel department's belief in the value of professionals, that they would often push certain occupations in the direction of increased professionalism.[43] Further, the recognition of professional groups by cities serves as a constant reminder to the personnel department of these interests, and therefore a constant institutional barrier to those wishing to alter the closed professional system.

Civil service systems were not created with the notion that municipal unions would exist as a participant in personnel policy.[44] In fact, municipal unions have obtained a great degree of control over many of the personnel processes affecting their members. These unions distribute large sums of city money for such personnel functions as health and life insurance, training, annuities, and counseling.[45] They have had considerable impact on the personnel system in their quest for greater control in the areas of recruitment, selection, position classification, promotion, training, discipline, and career development. Union policy has been to maintain the protective aspects of the merit system in the personnel departments, but to shift aspects of personnel function such as position classification and salary administration to the bargaining table.[46]

While most municipal unions demonstrate greater interest in promotion policies related to their current members than in hiring policies related to potential members, they do show considerable interest in the hiring process. These unions often resist the lowering of job qualifications or changes in examinations for entry-level jobs. Unions whose members are comprised mostly of middle-class whites are particularly reluctant to accept any change in entrance requirements to the civil service. During the Lindsay administration in New York City, attempts were made at recruiting minorities to civil service positions by making adjustments in the qualification requirements, and deemphasizing written exams. Most major municipal unions were vehemently opposed to such adjustments in the civil service requirements. However, in contrast, to this position, there are occasions when these unions are open to changing traditional merit procedures with regard to the personnel process. They become strong advocates with respect to promotion of their members "whereby seniority becomes a more important factor and merit examination scores become less important."[47]

The prevailing situation is that unions with the greatest impact on personnel department policy are those who most strongly advocate a status quo, or a closed door policy. Those with the least power are those most amenable to fundamental changes in the personnel system. They are also most often those in lower-level jobs with greater minority representation. The impact of collective bargaining on department of personnel activities in the interests of minorities is either minimal or negative,[48] and in such cases as police officer or firefighter positions, represent significant institutional barriers to minorities.[49]

It has been argued that the effectiveness of municipal unions as they now exist depends to a large extent upon civil service protections.[50] Thus, the compatibility of municipal unions with personnel department goals becomes evident. These goals, however, in maintaining a status quo closed personnel system are not compatible with eliminating institutional barriers that affect the success of minorities in the civil service system.

Mayoral Leadership

Most mayors in large cities have not been particularly effective at eliminating the structural barriers in municipal civil service systems, which preclude easy access and promotion opportunities for minorities and women in civil service jobs. For some mayors it is difficult to break through their entrenched city bureaucracies to effect change. Others do not have the inclination to promote reform of their merit system.

During the period that Robert F. Wagner was mayor of New York City, emphasis was placed on the merit system as a mechanism for choosing the most qualified persons for city government jobs. While a 1963 Brookings Institution study, commissioned by Wagner, criticized recruitment and qualification practices in the Department of Personnel, the Wagner administration continued these practices and defended its administration of the civil service system.[51] In contrast, his successor, John V. Lindsay, a reform mayor, was overtly critical of the merit system.[52]

While Wagner concentrated on new public service jobs to meet the needs of the minority unemployed, Lindsay criticized the merit system for its outdated rules and regulations that effectively excluded minorities from the public service. He attempted to reform the civil service system by establishing programs to (1) evaluate qualifications for entrance into the civil service in order to determine discriminatory practices affecting minorities, (2) make minorities more aware of job opportunities in the city workforce, and (3) establish training programs to prepare the educationally disadvantaged for civil service examinations.[53]

By 1970 it seemed that Lindsay was prepared to implement preferential treatment in hiring practices in an attempt to recruit more minorities for city jobs. Racial quotas, however, were not an option the Lindsay administration relied on in employment goals. In 1970 New York City was faced with reducing the government workforce due to the fiscal crisis. Thus, there were few gains to be obtained by Lindsay's debated hiring policy.[54]

On his first day at work after being elected mayor in 1974, Abraham Beame issued an executive order that required a city commissioner to choose the individual on the top of an eligible list for a civil service job. This provision changed the Lindsay administration rule whereby any one of the top three candidates from a list could be selected. Having been a career civil servant, Beame was committed to the status quo of the merit system.[55] The one-in-three rule offers better opportunity to appoint a minority person to a job as compared to filling the job with the top person on the list.

Mayor Edward I. Koch, elected in 1977, has not implemented changes that eliminate the structural barriers in civil service.

The opportunity for mayoral involvement in civil service policy depends to a large extent on the structure of politics of the city. In Chicago, Richard Daley clearly had the power to increase the recruitment of minorities in city jobs. On a day-to-day basis Daley reviewed all new city employees with the director of patronage. No one could begin work in Chicago without the mayor's knowledge.[56]

A 1980 study on politics in Detroit and Atlanta argues the significance of mayoral leadership in achieving affirmative action in civil service systems. The black mayors in these cities appointed black personnel directors, implemented special recruitment efforts within minority neighborhoods, reevaluated the selection procedures (which led to a decrease in the emphasis on written tests), and appointed greater numbers of black department heads who chose city employees from the civil service lists. Levels of minority employment in the Detroit and Atlanta city workforces increased significantly, suggesting that mayoral leadership in these cities had an impact on personnel practices and procedures.[57] Thus, despite existing civil service systems, it is possible for mayoral leadership to provide the impetus for such changes that would open civil service jobs to greater numbers of minorities. Greater potential for these changes exist when mayors designate their own appointees to civil service commissions and personnel directorships. Otherwise, conflicting goals between the mayor and the bureaucracy can prevent change.

QUALIFICATIONS, EXAMINATIONS, AND PROMOTIONS: A SYSTEM LACKING QUALITY AND EQUITY

For the last two decades, the public service, particularly at the state and local level, has been one of the fastest growing sectors of the employment market.[58] As such, it should have offered the greatest opportunity for minority employment. The data presented in this study demonstrate that this has not been the case. The reason for the inability of the public service to adapt to the needs of these groups lies in the rigid structure of the civil service system and the merit principles that underlie the system.

The civil service system was originally rationalized and developed to ensure fairness and equal access to government positions. The system, however, has not worked that way. The reason is that civil service institutions, which pretend to be neutral, are exclusionary. While public personnel systems exist at all levels of government with varying policies and procedures, all of them must relate to general processes including classification, compensation, recruitment, testing and selection, evaluation, promotion, transfer, termination of employment, and discipline.[59] Among the major institutional barriers to full participation of minority and female groups in municipal civil service are the job classifications, the credentialling requirements, and the examination process.

The position classification plan was developed as a mechanism for implementing the merit system. The merit system necessitated documentation on the responsibilities of various groups of positions and the qualification requirements attached to the positions. The civil service reformers believed that the notion of "equal pay for equal work" could be attained through classification. Classification was also viewed as a tool to promote greater economy and efficiency in government.[60]

The impact of the classification system on minority employment in cities can be seen through the recruitment process. Efforts by the recruitment divisions have been directed primarily at open competitive positions; programs to recruit for noncompetitive or exempt positions have been minimal. It is significant to note that minority representation is at its highest in noncompetitive positions. While this does not by itself prove that the efforts to recruit minorities for competitive positions are ineffective or nonexistent, it does suggest that the recruitment divisions can do more to recruit minorities to city employment.[61]

The fact that minorities tend to be represented to a higher

degree in noncompetitive positions than competitive positions does not bode well for their future mobility in the system. Noncompetitive positions generally bear neither tenure nor promotional opportunities.

Experience requirements associated with many positions often tend to discriminate against undereducated minorities attempting to enter the public service. Further, the educational requirements attached to certain positions tend to discriminate against minority group members who do not complete as many years in school as white persons. According to the 1980 census (see Table 1), 68 percent of whites 25 years old and over graduated from high school compared with only 56.3 percent of blacks and 35.4 percent of persons of Spanish origin in the same age group in the New York metropolitan area. Of those persons 25 years old and over in the New York area who were college graduates, 84.9 percent were white, 8.5 percent were black, and 3.7 percent were of Spanish origin. The data in Table 1 indicate similar education patterns among racial groups in New York State and the United States as a whole. It can be concluded from these figures that position classifications requiring completion of high school or college would exclude a higher percentage of blacks and persons of Spanish origin than whites. The discrepancy becomes more glaring when the requirement is a college degree.

The system of position classification has also resulted in sexual discrimination. Recent efforts to achieve pay equity have led to research and public hearings, which have exposed the fact that many positions held predominantly by women are graded lower and paid less than those positions held mostly by men, but with similar levels of responsibility.[62] Research conducted on the status of women in the New York State government workforce reflects similar patterns in comparison with the city, in that "women hold a healthy share of the State civil service jobs. Equality of employment, however, has not been achieved. Women are vastly over-represented in low-paid positions and are not moving up within the civil service system."[63]

As suggested, women hold a significant number of positions in civil service. In 1981, 48 percent of the New York State government workforce was composed of women, and 31 percent of the employees in the New York City mayoral agencies were

Table 1
Years of School Completed

	Whole Population	White	Black	Spanish Origin
United States				
Total persons	226,545,805	189,079,281	26,504,985	14,588,876
Years of school completed				
Persons 25 years old and over	132,775,652	114,301,249	13,189,216	6,726,556
Completed 4 years H.S.	45,691,481	40,628,258	3,802,235	1,607,312
1-3 years college	20,800,462	18,306,564	1,762,720	788,094
College 4 or more years	21,593,443	19,616,869	1,106,217	514,819
Percent H.S. graduates	66.3%	68.7%	50.6%	43.3%
New York State				
Total persons	17,558,072	14,033,411	2,407,435	1,657,417
Years of school completed				
Persons 25 years old and over	10,713,565	8,857,121	1,283,529	833,016
Completed 4 years H.S.	3,579,645	3,044,070	429,649	178,280
1-3 years college	1,510,394	1,277,514	177,065	78,713
College 4 or more years	2,000,258	1,785,384	121,757	54,900
Percent H.S. graduates	66.2%	68.9%	56.8%	37.4%

(SMSA) New York, N.Y.-N.J.

Total persons	9,120,347	6,162,494	1,946,057	1,492,559
Years of school completed				
Persons 25 years old and over	5,781,556	4,197,332	1,064,523	757,177
Completed 4 years H.S.	1,717,927	1,263,722	357,427	154,510
1-3 years college	763,910	574,305	140,548	69,563
College 4 or more years	1,194,331	1,014,129	101,259	44,018
Percent H.S. graduates	63.6%	68.0%	56.3%	35.4%

SOURCE: Department of Commerce, Bureau of the Census, 1980 Census of Population and Housing. Provisional Estimates of Social, Economic, and Housing Characteristics (Washington, D.C.: U.S. Government Printing Office, March 1982).

women.[64] The reason that women do poorly, given that so many of them are appointed to low paying entry-level positions with few career ladder opportunities, lies primarily in the structural differences between positions defined typically as "male" or "female."[65] This pattern is of concern since an underlying principle of democratic government is that it should be representative of the public it serves.

The examination process is probably the most critical factor affecting the access of minorities to civil service jobs. Women are affected as well by the examination process for entrance to certain job categories. The use of written examinations to measure the fitness of applicants for a position became commonplace at all levels of government.

These examinations, as the courts have demonstrated (see Chapter 4), do not satisfactorily measure the suitability of an applicant for a position or a current employee for a promotion. As a result, many individuals who would be exemplary employees due to experience or high motivation are excluded from obtaining a job. Despite this situation, personnel systems consistently attempt to rationalize their examination requirements. Data indicate, however, that such selection devices discriminate against members of minority groups and women.[66]

Considering the importance of the competitive examination, both in civil service ideology and practice, allegations that the examination system creates a major barrier to minority employment is an important consideration. The examination system on the surface appears to be quite fair; the job specification and examinations are based on a job analysis, the individuals are ranked according to their test scores, with one of the top three chosen for the job. However, if the procedure for the job analysis turns out to be meaningless, and the ranked scores do not necessarily represent corresponding skill levels, the process becomes a mere attempt at justifying traditional civil service ideology and serves as a screening-out process.

Beyond the question of job analysis, the examinations themselves are open to question on a number of different levels. The most basic question is whether competitive examinations are necessary or even desirable for different city positions. Clearly, the necessity for competitive examinations for positions that have no formal education or experience requirements and require no special skill is open to question.

An example can be observed when, in 1982, New York City threw out a civil service examination for park laborers after discovering that 800 of the 1,000 employees who took the test received scores too low to keep their positions. These individuals were probationary employees originally hired under the CETA (Comprehensive Employment and Training Act of 1973) Program. When the funds were discontinued, they were maintained on the city payroll. Fewer than one in five of these laborers received scores high enough to obtain a permanent civil service position for work they were already doing. The work included picking up trash, cutting grass, and feeding zoo animals.[67]

Beyond the question of the desirability of competitive examinations for city positions, the ranking process is also open to question. The notion that one candidate is better qualified to do the job than the next person when the score differences are decimal points or even several percentage points is absurd.

The system through which individuals are promoted in city civil service systems is generally a closed system. Promotion in the New York City civil service, for example, is generally by closed examination. A "closed" examination is limited to those who are currently employed in the civil service. This compares with an "open" examination which is open to persons not currently employed in the system.[68] While it is a positive force within an organization to promote people from within, this practice in the civil service system tends to be "an exclusionary device that limits competition," and "the worst feature of the promotion system is that an employee's chance of promotion bears no relation to his performance on the job."[69]

Considering the paramount importance of the examination process, it is not surprising that a number of legal actions have arisen, challenging specific examinations. It is interesting to note that these court actions are not challenges to the civil service system but rather to specific civil service provisions. In most instances those who have challenged examinations appear to have accepted the principles underlying the merit system. Several of these court cases are reviewed in Chapter 4.

As has been shown, aspects of the merit system relating to

qualifications, examinations, and promotions have formed institutional barriers which exclude minorities and women from pursuing successful careers in the civil service.

CONCLUSIONS

The practices and procedures in civil service systems as described in this chapter present obstacles for minorities and women in obtaining civil service appointments and successfully moving up the system's career ladder. Vested interests developed by personnel departments, professional organizations, and municipal unions to maintain the status quo have had an exclusionary effect on the attempt by newer groups to achieve similar status in civil service as compared with older immigrant groups.

There are those who believe that minorities, particularly blacks, are intellectually inferior and therefore do not achieve well on examinations.[70] This is an important allegation in view of the discussion that the examination system in municipal civil service systems has an exclusionary effect on the entrance and promotion of minorities in civil service. The combination, however, of examinations that are often culturally biased, entrance requirements that are unrelated to job performance, and inflated education qualifications for lower-level positions are some of the reasons that the municipal civil service system has a discriminatory impact on minorities.

While women are represented by significant numbers in civil service jobs, they are overrepresented in the low paying entry-level positions with limited career opportunities. There are often structural differences in job categories between positions defined typically as "male" or "female." The entrance requirements for the female job categories are often higher and offer fewer career ladder opportunities. Certain job category examinations and requirements, such as uniformed services, have a discriminatory impact on women (see Chapter 4 for a discussion of alleged discrimination in the New York City firefighters examination).

It is worthy of note that in the process of collecting data for this study the author observed that the data do not even focus on women in several of the research categories. In a few of the cases discussed in Chapter 4, for example, the courts did not provide data relating to how women performed on particular civil service examinations, but they provided the data for minorities.

There are those who oppose remedies to correct alleged discrimination of minorities in public employment. These individuals argue against the use of any kind of quotas to remedy the exclusionary aspects of municipal civil service systems as well as other institutions in society. They believe that the use of quotas and goals will create a condition of reverse discrimination (this subject is discussed in Chapter 3).[71]

Given the inflexibility of the structure of municipal civil service systems and their exclusionary impact on minorities and women, it is important for governments to restructure these systems or devise alternatives if civil service systems are to be representative of the population at all levels.[72] The argument against quotas and goals is clearly not compatible with these objectives.

The next three chapters examine challenges to municipal civil service systems in the form of affirmative action programs, legal action, and public employment programs to determine their effectiveness in providing greater access by minorities and women to civil service jobs.

NOTES

1. Edward C. Banfield and James Q. Wilson, *City Politics* (New York: Vintage Books, 1963).

2. Robert M. Fogelson, *The Fragmented Metropolis: Los Angeles 1850–1930* (Cambridge, Mass.: Harvard University Press, 1967), p. 218.

3. James C. Renick, "The Impact of Municipal Affirmative Action Programs on Black Representation in Government Employment: Reality or Rhetoric?" *Southern Review of Public Administration* 5 (Summer 1981): 142, 145.

4. Frank J. Thompson, "Meritocracy, Equality and Employment: Commitment to Minority Hiring Among Public Officials," paper presented at the 1976 Annual Meeting of the American Political Science Association, Chicago, 2–5 September 1976, p. 2.

5. Ibid., p. 4.

6. Stephen M. David and Paul E. Peterson, eds., *Urban Politics and*

Public Policy: The City in Crisis (New York: Praeger Publishers, 1973), p. xii.

7. See David B. Truman, *The Governmental Process: Political Interests and Public Opinion* (New York: Alfred A. Knopf, 1951); Edward C. Banfield, *Political Influence: A New Theory of Urban Politics* (New York: The Free Press, 1961).

8. Randall B. Ripley and Grace A. Franklin, *Bureaucracy and Policy Implementation* (Homewood, Ill.: The Dorsey Press, 1982), pp. 12–13.

9. Robert A. Caro, *The Power Broker: Robert Moses and the Fall of New York* (New York: Alfred A. Knopf, 1974), pp. 52–63; and Robert Moses, *The Civil Service of Great Britain* (New York: Columbia University, 1914). For a historical analysis of the development of the public administration movement in America, see Dwight Waldo, *The Administrative State: A Study of the Political Theory of American Public Administration* (New York: The Ronald Press Company, 1948).

10. O. Glenn Stahl, *Public Personnel Administration* (New York: Harper & Row, 1971), p. 355.

11. David L. Martin, *Running City Hall: Municipal Administration in America* (University, Ala.: The University of Alabama Press, 1982), p. 122.

12. Jacob J. Rutstein, "Survey of Current Personnel Systems in State and Local Governments," *Good Government*, Spring 1971, pp. 1–2.

13. Urban Data Service, Andrew Boesel, "Civil Service Commissions in City and County Government" (Washington, D.C.: International City Management Association, vol. 5, no. 6, June 1973), p. 1.

14. Donald E. Klingner, "Political Influences on the Design of State and Local Personnel Systems," *Review of Public Personnel Administration* 1 (Summer 1981): 9.

15. Grace Hall Saltzstein, "Personnel Directors and Female Employment Representation: A New Addition to Models of Equal Employment Opportunity Policy?" *Social Science Quarterly* 64 (December 1983): 734–746.

16. Edith Baikie, *Civil Service in the City of New York: A Study of the Operations of the Municipal Civil Service Commission with Recommended Reforms* (New York: Citizens Budget Commission, 1938).

17. Wallace S. Sayre and Herbert Kaufman, *Governing New York City: Politics in the Metropolis* (New York: W. W. Norton & Company, 1965), p. 383; New York City, Mayor's Committee on Management Survey, *Modern Management for the City of New York*, 2 vols. (New York: The Committee, 1953); and Temporary State Commission to Study the Organizational Structure of the Government of the City of New York (Josephs Commission), *Four Steps to Better Government of New York City: A Plan for Action*, 2 vols. (New York: The Commission, 1953).

18. In order for the doctrine of equal pay for equal work to be followed, the reformers believed that what was needed was a detailed set of job descriptions (and job requirements) for all city positions.

19. Sayre and Kaufman, *Governing New York City*, p. 382.

20. New York City, Office of the Mayor, Executive Order 49, 31 March 1958.

21. New York City, Department of Personnel, *Annual Report(s)*, 1958–1964.

22. In 1963, a Brookings Institution study concluded that classification specifications needed to be completely revamped in order to distinguish one level from another in the professional, technical, and managerial levels in the city workforce; David T. Stanley, *Higher Skills for the City of New York: Report of Study of Professional, Technical, and Managerial Manpower Needs of the City of New York* (Washington, D.C.: The Brookings Institution, March 1963), pp. 306–316; and in 1966 the Mayor's Task Force on City Personnel, found that "the classification plan and the pay plan of the City are out of date. They have been virtually destroyed by years of ad hoc changes." *Report of the Mayor's Task Force on City Personnel*, New York City, 3 May 1966, p. 18.

23. New York City, Office of the Mayor, Personnel Implementing Order 21/67, 15 March 1967.

24. Ralph Blumenthal, "Necessity of Civil Service Questioned in City Report," *New York Times*, 16 November 1972, p. 1.

25. State Charter Revision Commission for New York City, *Personnel Reforms for New York City, Staff Recommendations*, Part I, New York City, January 1975, p. 3.

26. Ibid., p. 56.

27. Ibid., pp. 56–61; New York City, Department of Personnel, *City-Wide Charter Implementation Plan*, New York City, December 1976; and New York City, Department of Personnel, *Rules and Regulations of the City Personnel Director*, New York City, 19 July 1978.

28. New York City, Department of Personnel, *City-Wide Charter Implementation Plan*, pp. A1–A2.

29. State Charter Revision Commission for New York City, *Final Report of the State Charter Revision Commission for New York City*, New York City, n.d., p. 9.

30. National Academy of Public Administration, *A Review of the Philadelphia Civil Service System: Design for Accountability* (Washington, D.C.: National Academy of Public Administration, July 1981), pp. ii–iv.

31. Ibid., pp. 46–47.

32. Ibid., pp. 48–49.

33. Interview with Harry I. Bronstein, Director of the New York City

Department of Personnel and Chairman of the New York City Civil Service Commission, 12 September 1973.

34. Douglas M. Fox, *The Politics of City and State Bureaucracy* (Pacific Palisades, Calif.: Goodyear, 1974), p. 19, quoted in Harold F. Gortner, *Administration in the Public Sector* (New York: John Wiley & Sons, 1977), pp. 65–66.

35. Gortner, *Administration in the Public Sector*, p. 66.

36. Dennis F. Thompson, *John Stuart Mill and Representative Government* (Princeton, N.J.: Princeton University Press, 1976), p. 66.

37. Ibid., p. 68.

38. Frederick C. Mosher, *Democracy and the Public Service*, 2nd ed. (New York: Oxford University Press, 1982), pp. 133–134.

39. Sayre and Kaufman, *Governing New York City*, pp. 385–386.

40. Ibid., p. 74.

41. Frederick M. Wirt, *Power in the City: Decision Making in San Francisco* (Berkeley, Calif.: University of California Press, 1974), p. 311; for a further discussion of licensing and standards of professionals in public employment see Mosher, *Democracy and the Public Service*, 2nd ed., pp. 137–142.

42. Ibid., p. 18.

43. New York City, Department of Personnel, *Annual Report(s)*, 1954–1959.

44. Mosher, *Democracy and the Public Service*, 2nd ed., p. 188.

45. Solomon Hoberman, "Personnel Management and Labor Relations in New York City," in State Charter Revision Commission, *Personnel Reforms for New York City*, p. 18.

46. Sterling D. Spero and John M. Capozzola, *The Urban Community and Its Unionized Bureaucracies: Pressure Politics in Local Government Relations* (New York: Dunnellen Publishing Company, 1973), pp. 173, 209.

47. Raymond D. Horton, *Municipal Labor Relations in New York City: Lessons of the Lindsay-Wagner Years* (New York: Praeger Publishers, 1972), pp. 112–113; see also David T. Stanley, *Managing Local Government Under Union Pressure* (Washington, D.C.: The Brookings Institution, 1972), pp. 32–49; and Ewart Guinier, "Impact of Unionization on Blacks," in *Unionization of Municipal Employees*, Proceedings of the Academy of Political Science (New York, Columbia University, Vol. 30, 1970): 173–181.

48. Horton, *Municipal Labor Relations in New York City*, pp. 112–113.

49. William B. Gould, "Labor Relations and Race Relations," in *Public Workers and Public Unions*, ed. Sam Zagoria (Englewood Cliffs, N.J.: Prentice-Hall, 1972), pp. 156–157.

50. Emma Schweppe, *The Firemen's and Patrolmen's Unions in the City of New York: A Case Study in Public Employee Unions* (New York: King's Crown Press, 1948), p. 49.

51. Joseph P. Viteritti, *Bureaucracy and Social Justice: The Allocation of Jobs and Services to Minority Groups* (Port Washington, N.Y.: Kennikat Press, 1979), pp. 66–67.

52. Ibid., p. 68.

53. Ibid.

54. Ibid., p. 71.

55. Murrray Schumach, "Beame Says Aides Must Hew to Line on Civil Service," *New York Times*, 3 January 1974, p. 1.

56. Mike Royko, *Boss: Richard J. Daley of Chicago* (New York: E. P. Dutton & Company, 1971), p. 17.

57. Peter K. Eisinger, "Black Employment in Municipal Jobs: The Impact of Black Political Power," *The American Political Science Review* 76 (June 1982): 382.

58. From 1967 to 1982, the New York State government workforce increased from 171,102 to 254,181 employees. During the same period, the local government workforce in New York State increased from 745,979 to 866,702 employees. U.S. Department of Commerce, Bureau of the Census, *1967 Census of Governments. Public Employment* (Washington, D.C.: U.S. Government Printing Office, 1969); and U.S. Department of Commerce, Bureau of the Census, *Public Employment in 1982* (Washington, D.C.: U.S. Government Printing Office, 1983).

59. Gortner, *Administration in the Public Sector*, p. 274.

60. Ibid., p. 275.

61. Interview with Morris B. Schiechel, Director, Bureau of Recruitment and Employee Incentive, and Nelson Dworkin, Chief, Recruitment Division, New York City Department of Personnel, 24 October 1973 and 27 November 1973.

62. Elizabeth Weiner, "No More Cheap Women," *Village Voice*, 13 March 1984, p. 5.

63. Sandra Peterson-Hardt and Nancy D. Perlman, *Sex-Segregated Career Ladders in New York State Government: A Structural Analysis of Inequality in Employment* (Albany, N.Y.: Center for Women in Government, State University of New York at Albany, October 1979), p. 1.

64. Lillie McLaughlin, *Detailed Statistics on Women and Minorities in New York State and New York City Government Employment: 1981–1982* (Albany, N.Y.: Center for Women in Government, State University of New York at Albany, Spring 1983), pp. 1, 6.

65. Peterson-Hardt and Perlman, *Sex-Segregated Career Ladders in New York State Government*, pp. 1–3, 18, 82–83; see "Women's Center Study: State Pay System Hurting Minorities," *The Chief*, 27 February 1987, p. 1, for the results of a study indicating that New York State job titles held mostly by blacks, Hispanics, and women pay an average of 15

percent less than positions with similar job qualifications held by white males.

66. E. Richard Larson, "Discriminatory Selection Devices in Public Employment Systems," *Good Government*, Winter 1971, pp. 1–3.

67. Maurice Carroll, "Scores Low, City Ends Civil Service Test," *New York Times*, 9 December 1982, p. Bl.

68. Gortner, *Administration in the Public Sector*, p. 283.

69. E. S. Savas and Sigmund G. Ginsberg, "The Civil Service: A Meritless System," *The Public Interest*, no. 32 (Summer 1973): 77–78.

70. For a discussion and refutation of this argument see Philip Green, *The Pursuit of Inequality* (New York: Pantheon Books, 1981).

71. Nathan Glazer, *Affirmative Discrimination: Ethnic Inequality and Public Policy* (New York: Basic Books, 1975; Harper Colophon Books, 1978), pp. ix–xix.

72. In thinking about the impact of current practices and procedures in civil service it is worthy of note that a study of affirmative action and local government employment in Dallas concluded that the existing non–civil service system "was capable of responding to affirmative action guidelines quicker than a civil service system." Dallas has two different civil service systems for the purpose of recruiting and promoting city employees. The majority of city departments function within the first, a traditional civil service system. Eight departments and one-third of the municipal employees in Dallas are exempt by the city charter from civil service regulations. They function under their own, less rigid systems of recruitment, hiring, and promotion. Christine Wicker and Mark S. Rosentraub, "Affirmative Action and Local Government Employment: A Case Study of Institutional Response by Civil Service and Non-Civil Service Departments," in *Public Administration and Public Policy: A Minority Perspective*, eds. Lawrence C. Howard, Lenneal J. Henderson, Jr., and Deryl G. Hunt (Pittsburgh: Public Policy Press, 1977), p. 331.

Challenges to the Merit System: Affirmative Action

3

In examining efforts to achieve social equity in municipal civil service systems, one must look at the development of civil service systems at various levels and the various programs designed for that purpose. Many of these programs were created to recruit minority groups to the public service. They emerged in response to charges of discrimination in the regular civil service system. Data indicated that, although the civil service served as an important source of minority employment as compared to the private sector, the number of minority people in such systems was minimal.[1] In the 1960s, local councils of OEO (Office of Economic Opportunity) organizations, for example, looked to civil service as a means of creating a noncompetitive route to jobs. The potential beneficiaries of these poverty programs, however, were quickly disillusioned by the inability of the civil service system to create sufficient employment mobility for the poor.[2] From 1961 to the present, affirmative action programs increased the total number of minority employees and their representation in intermediate- and higher-level positions, but they have not produced equal representation at the higher-level positions.[3]

Such legislation as the Equal Employment Opportunity Act

of 1972 and attempts at creating institutional mechanisms to promote affirmative action lend themselves to evaluating whether or not they have achieved the goal of bureaucratic representation. It has been suggested that inherent in the goals of affirmative action reforms is the expansion in relative proportions of underrepresented groups in the bureaucracy.[4]

Achieving the goal of social equity requires not just changing the law, but changing the attitudes and structural barriers existing in institutions in our society. Many of these changes are antithetical to the goals of personnel professionals in civil service systems, who rationalize existing structures in terms of the values of efficiency and expertise.

Attempts at implementing affirmative action programs often spur the escalation of social issues: (1) the difference between affirmative action and "nondiscrimination"; (2) the importance of preferential hiring and the establishment of target quotas in the affirmative action process; and (3) the need for reexamination of traditional standards of "quality."[5]

Despite opposition[6] and attempts to block affirmative action, between 1960 and the present, various legislative and legal actions have been initiated with the intent of implementing affirmative action. Some of these efforts will be examined later in this chapter. Meeting affirmative action requirements, for example, was a prerequisite for localities to participate in many federal grant programs.

Efforts to enhance the cause of affirmative action have received little assistance from the Ronald Reagan administration. If anything, the country is experiencing retrenchment with this administration. President Reagan has indicated that he opposes affirmative action. In its attempt to reduce federal regulation, for example, the Reagan administration moved to relax antidiscrimination rules for federal contractors and to ease requirements for remedial action. "The proposals would eliminate the requirement for a review of an employer's hiring patterns before a Federal contract is awarded, for example, and, in the construction trades, would reduce the number of affirmative action steps required of contractors."[7]

A further illustration of the Reagan administration stand on affirmative action occurred in 1985, when the Justice Department argued before the Supreme Court that affirmative action plans that give preferential treatment to minority group members violate the Constitution. In contrast to the Carter administration, the Reagan administration does not have an affirmative action program to increase minorities and women in senior managerial positions in government.[8]

Achieving affirmative action is no simple task. Many suggest that government must take an active role in order to guarantee a representative, competent workforce for the public service. Representativeness and competence are compatible notions, which are mutually reinforcing. The challenge of affirmative action is in integrating the notions of representativeness and competence.[9]

AFFIRMATIVE ACTION PROGRAMS

This study examines the affirmative action legislation that resulted from debates concerning merit and social equity. The resulting legislation has led to additional debate and controversy, lawsuits, and proposals for modified legislation. Attitudes and reactions of personnel professionals toward implementation of affirmative action programs will also be viewed.

Affirmative Action Legislation

It is worth noting that public action came with regulation of the public sector. A major effort to eliminate discrimination occurred with the passage of the Civil Rights Act of 1964. The Equal Employment Opportunity Commission (EEOC) and Title VII, which gave EEOC the power to bring suit involving cases of discrimination in private employment, were established as a result of the Civil Rights Act. The act also reasserted the non-discrimination policy in federal employment. Further, in 1965 President Lyndon Johnson issued Executive Order 11246 prohibiting discrimination involving federal contracts. The order also prohibited discrimination in federal employment. In 1967, Executive Order 11375 extended coverage to discrimination based on sex.[10]

Local government employment was not initially covered under the Civil Rights Act of 1964. In 1969, the U.S. Commission on Civil Rights surveyed state and local agencies in several large metropolitan areas to determine the extent of minority employment in public service on the state and local levels. The survey concluded that minorities were denied equal access to government employment. The Commission recommended "(1) that the Civil Rights Act of 1964 be amended to make all state and local governments subject to its provisions and (2) that each locality adopt a program of employment equality to assure nondiscrimination in current practices."[11]

While neither of these proposals was implemented specifically, there were a few occurrences which prodded state and local governments to make efforts in assuring equal employment opportunity in their personnel systems. The Intergovernmental Personnel Act of 1970, for example, established " 'fair treatment' as a policy for all governments receiving funds to expand and improve merit systems." In addition,

the Equal Employment Opportunity Act of 1972 made almost all local governments subject to the antidiscrimination provisions of Title VII of the 1964 Civil Rights Act. Discrimination in government employment on the basis of race, color, sex, religion, or national origin was forbidden and legal remedies were provided.[12]

It should be noted that the term affirmative action was used for the first time in Executive Order 10925, issued by President John F. Kennedy, which established the President's Committee on Equal Employment Opportunity. President Johnson issued probably the most important executive order regarding affirmative action, Executive Order 11246. This order emphasized a policy of nondiscrimination in federal employment and called for the establishment of affirmative action programs.[13]

The 1972 legislation, however, was said to be ineffective. But important changes in the federal government's approach to antidiscrimination were implemented in President Carter's 1978 Reorganization Plan. The plan reassigned equal employment duties among various federal agencies.[14]

Responsibility for affirmative action is assigned to individual agencies. Each agency is responsible for developing central agency and regional affirmative action plans. The Civil Service Commission had responsibility for setting standards and reviewing plans, but under the Carter reorganization, responsibility for standards shifted to the Equal Employment Opportunity Commission, and agency plans are filtered through the Office of Personnel Management. EEOC has the power to review agency actions implemented in accordance with their affirmative action plans.[15] In the past, the Civil Service Commission had responsibility for reviewing state and local agency plans, but as with the federal agencies, the 1978 reorganization shifted the responsibility to the EEOC.[16]

Most affirmative action plans have a similar format. They include, for example, a policy statement supporting affirmative action, identification of existing discriminatory patterns, and characteristics of the agency workforce as compared with the availability pool of the immediate labor market. Ideally, successful implementation of affirmative action would stress recruitment of persons who have been underrepresented in the government workforce and then working to develop their skills and career opportunities in the public service.[17]

Given the important role of affirmative action in the process of recruiting minorities and women to civil service positions, it is essential to analyze the attitudes concerning affirmative action by personnel professionals responsible for the implementation of affirmative action plans.

Personnel Professionals and Affirmative Action

Research dealing with the attitude of public officials toward hiring minorities indicates that personnel administrators are among the most critical participants in the decision-making process influencing recruitment to government positions.[18] In 1975, a survey was conducted of 1,506 personnel administrators to determine their commitment with regard to minority hiring. Of the respondents, 65 percent were employed by local government, 28 percent by the state, and 7 percent by the federal government.[19]

The findings are significant since they demonstrate that those officials who develop an attitudinal commitment to hiring minorities are more likely to translate that commitment into behavior. So, for instance, personnel administrators with attitudinal commitments toward hiring minorities are more likely to launch programs to do so. Such officials who act positively about recruiting minorities are less likely to advocate increased credential or experience requirements for positions.[20]

While most of the respondents in this survey believe that public agencies should advertise and recruit actively for minorities, and that where competence is about equal they would encourage hiring a minority over a white applicant, they overwhelmingly believe that if a more competent white applicant is available, he or she should receive priority in hiring over a minority.[21]

The study suggests that personnel officials who are minority, female, younger, from a higher-class background, and who grew up in more urbanized areas would lend support to appointing minorities. But those officials who are white, male, and/or older are less committed to employing minorities.[22]

Officials who think that hiring minorities will lower the level of competence in government will most likely not actively recruit minorities. Personnel administrators who follow the traditional merit principle which declares that government should hire the most competent people available are likely to respond negatively to recruiting minorities.[23]

The results of the survey of personnel administrators suggests that the greatest degree of variance concerning equality can be explained by beliefs concerning organizational trade-offs and sociopolitical beliefs. In addition, three variables are particularly important predictors of greater commitment by personnel administrators to hiring minorities: negative perception of the status of blacks in society, positive attitude concerning the contribution of minorities as employees on government competence, and a pledge to economic equality.[24] Finally, it appears that "political liberalism" of personnel administrators plays a significant role in their attitudes toward implementing affirmative action programs, and, furthermore, that this political ideology is a greater significant factor than "outside socio-political pressures."[25]

Another study of personnel policy in Oakland, California, has focused on the recruitment process. In an attempt to recruit more minorities in the Oakland fire department, staff members made exerted efforts to attract minority applicants. And, in fact, the 220 minority applicants who took the exam represented ten times the number who took the exam the last time it was taken. More than one-third of those taking the test were minorities. While the process to get minority applicants may have been successful, the examination phase was not.[26] Twenty-three percent of the whites passed all phases of the test, but only 6 percent of the minorities passed. While the personnel director acted in response to poor minority representation in the fire department by incorporating minor adjustments in a broad range of recruitment devices, it is questionable whether these changes would translate into more minority employees. Many of the changes he made, in fact, were not successful at increasing minority hiring.[27]

It is worthy of note that, in an interview concerning recruitment of minorities in a New York City agency, the supervisor believed (despite acknowledgment of the discriminatory aspects of the civil service system) that if agencies are committed to hiring at least a small number of minorities, it is possible.[28]

The chief of the Affirmative Action Division in the Los Angeles City Attorney's Office expressed an interesting attitude about that office as having a basic conflict in legal responsibilities as they relate to discrimination. She observes that the office has an obligation to defend city departments against legal challenges to policy with alleged discriminatory aspects. It is also, however, the responsibility of the City Attorney to protect the electorate in terms of their legal rights. Therefore, the City Attorney would be obligated to work with city agencies in dismantling institutional barriers which preclude equal employment access to women and minorities in city government.[29]

In evaluating efforts and devising strategies to achieve affirmative action it is important to recognize that support remains strong for the values of meritocracy, despite pleas for social equity. Significant numbers of personnel officials still believe strongly in the traditional merit precept that government should hire the most competent persons available. Thus, those personnel administrators who see no conflict between hiring minorities and maintaining the values of meritocracy are those most likely to dedicate themselves to affirmative action.[30]

It is important to examine to what extent affirmative action programs have affected the distribution of minorities and women employed by government. An article in the *Wall Street Journal*, ten years after "goals and timetables" were mandated by federal guidelines, suggests that while affirmative action "demands hard statistical results from others," in fact, the program has not achieved positive results for the disadvantaged minorities.[31]

MINORITIES AND WOMEN IN GOVERNMENT EMPLOYMENT

This study has previously focused on the notion that public service employment continues to be discussed as a viable mechanism for alleviating problems of unemployment despite the constraints which been imposed on open recruitment into civil service systems. (Table 2 illustrates the growth of public sector employment from 1939 to 1986 on the federal, state, and local levels.) Minorities and women are, traditionally, the groups hardest hit by increased unemployment. Empirical data, however, can reveal the extent to which current civil service systems institutionally discriminate against these groups.

While the prime interest of this study is on municipal civil service, it would seem relevant for comparative purposes to examine how minorities have fared in the federal and state civil service systems as well. Representative data relating to state and city governments are utilized, with New York State and New York City used as prime examples.

Research indicates that analysis of affirmative action data relating to municipal government workforces is limited. The EEOC, which maintains responsibility for monitoring affirmative action plans at the municipal level, underutilizes the data it does collect from local governments.[32]

It also appears that the majority of research on affirmative action programs has dealt with federal employees. This is partly due to the accessibility of data on the federal level, partly to the

Table 2
Public Sector Employment for Selected Years, Annual Averages (in Thousands)

Year	Government Employment	Federal	State	Local
1939	3,995	905	3,090[a]	
1944	6,043	2,928	3,116[a]	
1949	5,856	1,908	3,948[a]	
1954	6,751	2,188	4,563[a]	
1959	8,083	2,233	1,484	4,366
1964	9,596	2,348	1,856	5,392
1969	12,195	2,758	2,533	6,904
1974	14,170	2,724	3,039	8,407
1979	15,947	2,866	3,541	9,633
1980	16,241	2,866	3,610	9,765
1981	16,024	2,772	3,623	9,629
1982	15,632	2,735	3,499	9,245
1983	16,115	2,751	3,735	9,629
1984	16,146	2,768	3,777	9,601
1985	16,489	2,819	3,886	9,784
1986	16,948	2,898	4,014	10,036

SOURCE: U.S. Department of Labor, Employment and Earnings, United States, 1909-78, Bulletin 1322-22, 2979; Supplement to Employment and Earnings Revised Establishment Data, June 1982; U.S. Department of Labor, Supplement to Employment and Earnings: Supplement to Employment, Hours, and Earnings, United States, 1909-84, Revised Establishment Data, June 1986, pp. 188-189; and Employment and Earnings, Table B-2, various months, in Charles L. Betsey, "Minority Participation in the Public Sector" (Washington, D.C.: The Urban Institute, November 1982), p. 5. (Mimeographed paper.)

[a]Separate detail for state and local government employment is not available before 1955.

fact that the laws and regulations governing affirmative action emanate from the federal level.[33] This study attempts to contribute to the needed analysis of affirmative action data at the local level.

Analysis of affirmative action data at any level of government must be set in a comparative context. Any adequate exploration of the discriminatory effects of governmental personnel policies must revolve around two basic questions in order to establish a comparative framework: (1) What is the extent of minority representation in the government workforce? and (2) What is the nature of this representation in terms of the nature of the job and salary levels?

Minorities and Women in the Federal Government

In 1967, Cummings, Jennings, and Kilpatrick did a comparison of minority employment in the federal workforce with similar data on the general workforce in the United States. They found that whereas 11 percent of the United States workforce were nonwhite, 21 percent of the federal workforce were minority group members. In 1970, Hellriegel and Short discovered that the percentage of black government workers exceeded their ratio in the general population by 15 percent.[34]

A short time later Nachmias and Rosenbloom completed a more extensive study of the ethnicity of federal employees by agency and grade. While they also found that minorities were well represented in federal jobs, they discovered significant differences among various agencies and representation by minorities to be lower at higher grade levels.[35] Agencies with responsibility primarily for social-related programs, such as the EEOC and the Departments of Labor, Health, Education, and Welfare (HEW), and Housing and Urban Development (HUD), were found to employ the highest percentage of minorities. Moreover, Hispanics, American Indians, and Orientals were found to be more poorly represented in federal government jobs than were blacks.[36]

An extensive study of public employment in the United States was conducted by Harry Kranz in 1976. Kranz compared employment data on the federal, state, and local levels. His research supports previous federal studies, and, further, upholds these patterns at all levels of government. Given these consistencies, however, Kranz does find differences in minority representation to exist among the federal, state, and local levels of government. Minorities were found to be better represented in federal employment than at state or township levels, but they were best represented at county and city government levels. Kranz also discovered variances within the same levels of government in different geographical areas. Thus, the research demonstrated that while minorities in California and Alaska had the same representation in the general population (22.9 percent and 22.7 percent, respectively), minorities were represented in federal employment in California by more than twice their numbers in Alaska (26.5 percent compared with 11.5 percent).[37]

As noted earlier, federal, state, and local governments are similar in their composition of minorities and women in the workforce. Table 3 illustrates that in 1975 government employees consisted of about 20 percent minorities and about 35 percent women.[38] A comparison with 1985 data in the same table shows small increases for minorities and women in the federal, state, and local governments. It is worth noting, however, that the greatest growth in public employment has been in state and local governments rather than the federal government (see Table 2).

In another study of blacks in federal employment, research concludes that the proportion of blacks in lower-level grades with low salaries is greater than their representation in the federal service. Also, in comparing grade and salary ranges in the federal government between May 1972 and May 1974, the researchers observed significant impact of the Equal Employment Opportunity Act of 1972.[39]

Minorities and Women in State and Local Government

Similar patterns exist at the state and local levels as compared to the federal government. As of 1975, the median salary for a white worker in comparable jobs in state and local government was $10,167. The median salary for minorities was $8,788. Males were higher salaried than females ($11,295, compared with

Table 3
Percentage Distribution of Minorities and Women in Federal, and
State and Local Positions, 1975–1985

	1975 Positions		1985 Positions	
	Federal	State and Local	Federal	State and Local
Minorities	21.0	20.4	26.0	24.8
Blacks	15.9	15.4	17.6	17.6
Hispanics	3.3	3.8	4.5	5.2
Native Americans	0.9	0.3	1.0	0.5
Oriental Americans	0.9	0.7	2.9	1.5
Women	35.3	37.5	37.4	41.2

SOURCE: Robert D. Lee, Jr., Public Personnel Systems
(Baltimore: University Park Press, 1979), p. 243; U.S.
Equal Opportunity Commission, Annual Report on the Employment
of Minorities, Women and Handicapped Individuals in the
Federal Government, Fiscal Year 1985 (Washington, D.C.:
U.S. Government Printing Office, June 1987); and U.S. Equal
Employment Opportunity Commission, "Minorities and Women
in State and Local Government, 1985" (Washington, D.C.:
U.S. Government Printing Office, 1987).

$8,178). Minorities were employed in approximately 8 percent of the highest paying state and local jobs ($25,000 or more).[40] A comparison with 1980 shows similarities in the pattern of salary distribution in state and local government employment. The median salary for a white worker was $13,802, while blacks earned $11,501. Males also earned higher incomes than females, $15,159, compared with $11,414. Eighty-nine percent of the highest paying state and local jobs ($25,000 or more) were held by males (78.1 percent were white males and 8.5 percent were females, while only 9.5 percent were blacks).[41]

Data also indicate that minorities and women are concentrated in certain occupations. Table 4 shows the distribution of minor-

Table 4
Percentage Distribution of Minorities and Women in State and Local Government by Occupation, 1975–1985

Occupation	1975 Minorities		1975 Women		1985 Minorities		1985 Women	
	As Percent of Occupation	As Percent of Total	As Percent of Occupation	As Percent of Total	As Percent of Occupation	As Percent of Total	As Percent of Occupation	As Percent of Total
Officials and administrators	8.3	2.0	18.9	2.5	12.3	2.6	28.0	3.6
Professionals	12.8	11.1	39.8	18.7	18.4	14.9	46.9	22.9
Technicians	15.2	7.2	32.2	8.3	20.4	8.2	39.5	9.5
Protective service workers	12.2	8.0	5.9	2.1	19.1	11.8	9.5	3.5
Paraprofessionals	34.6	15.4	66.9	16.3	36.8	11.5	70.6	13.3
Office and clerical	19.6	18.7	83.8	43.4	26.7	19.8	87.8	39.3
Skilled craft workers	16.0	6.6	5.1	1.1	21.1	7.1	3.7	0.7

Table 4 (*Continued*)

| | 1975 | | | | 1985 | | | |
| | Minorities | | Women | | Minorities | | Women | |
Occupation	As Percent of Occupation	As Percent of Total	As Percent of Occupation	As Percent of Total	As Percent of Occupation	As Percent of Total	As Percent of Occupation	As Percent of Total
Service-maintenance	36.6	31.0	16.4	7.6	40.6	24.1	19.6	7.0
Total	100.0	100.0	100.0	100.0	100.0	100.0	100.0	99.8[a]

SOURCE: U.S. Equal Employment Opportunity Commission, Minorities and Women in State and Local Government, 1975, vol. I (Washington, D.C.: U.S. Government Printing Office, 1977), pp. 1-9, 177. Data based upon 2,387 jurisdictions, cited in Robert D. Lee, Jr., Public Personnel Systems (Baltimore: University Park Press, 1979), p. 244; U.S. Equal Employment Opportunity Commission, "Minorities and Women in State and Local Government, 1985" (Washington, D.C.: U.S. Government Printing Office, 1987).

[a]varies due to rounding.

ities and women in state and local government by occupation for 1975 and 1985. In 1975 more than 80 percent of the clerical jobs were held by women; clerical positions represented more than 40 percent of all state and local jobs held by women. Women also held a significant percentage of the paraprofessional jobs. In contrast, minorities held large numbers of service-maintenance jobs. Almost 20 percent of all administrators were female. This compares with only 8 percent of the administrators who were minority group members as of 1975.[42] By 1985 this representation had increased by four percentage points.

Table 5 illustrates that minorities and women are concentrated in some departments and functional areas. More than half of the state and local government employees in the areas of financial administration, public welfare, hospitals and sanitariums, health, and employment security were women in 1975 and 1985. Women held more than 60 percent of all positions in the functional areas of welfare, health, and hospitals. The data further indicate that in 1975 minority group members accounted for more than 40 percent of the jobs in the housing and sanitation/sewage fields, and approximately 25 percent of all jobs in hospitals. In 1975 minorities, however, did not hold a majority of jobs in any functional area. Moreover, in 1985, minorities still held under 40 percent of the jobs except in housing and sanitation.[43]

The patterns observed in the distribution of jobs can in part be explained by educational background. It has been suggested, for example, that certain disciplines such as civil engineering have few women graduates and thus, state agencies might have difficulty in recruiting women with that expertise. In addition, since greater numbers of whites attend college than minorities, whites have an advantage in gaining high-level jobs.[44] Recent data do not indicate a promising trend. While the period between 1960 and 1980 reflected increases in the number of blacks enrolled in colleges, the latest federal figures show a decline in the number of blacks enrolled in colleges both in real numbers and as a percentage of all college students.[45] This highlights the importance of equal opportunity for minorities and women in education.

Examination of the racial and sexual composition of state and

Table 5
Percentage Distribution of Minorities and Women in State and
Local Government by Functional Area, 1975–1985

Function	1975				1985			
	Minorities		Women		Minorities		Women	
	As Percent of Function	As Percent of Total	As Percent of Function	As Percent of Total	As Percent of Function	As Percent of Total	As Percent of Function	As Percent of Total
Financial administration	13.6	8.2	51.5	16.8	21.8	11.3	56.7	18.3
Streets and highways	12.5	7.4	8.4	2.7	18.8	6.4	13.4	2.8
Public welfare	26.2	9.8	72.9	14.8	33.0	8.9	74.6	12.5
Police protection	11.0	5.9	14.0	4.1	18.2	7.2	21.?	5.4
Fire protection	6.7	1.4	1.6	0.2	13.6	2.1	3.7	0.3
Natural resources	17.2	4.4	19.8	2.8	21.4	4.1	25.3	3.0
Hospitals and sanitariums	29.6	25.5	70.2	32.9	33.4	21.2	72.6	28.6
Health	21.8	5.9	63.7	9.5	27.8	6.5	67.9	9.8

Housing	42.7	3.6	26.9	1.2	50.0	3.2	32.1	1.3
Community development	18.8	0.8	32.3	0.8	22.2	0.8	42.7	1.0
Corrections	20.7	4.4	27.9	3.2	28.5	7.1	30.2	4.6
Utilities and transportation	26.8	9.8	12.1	2.4	36.5	11.0	17.6	3.3
Sanitation and sewage	40.1	7.2	3.4	0.3	40.5	4.6	8.6	0.6
Employment security	18.6	1.9	56.7	3.2	25.9	1.8	61.6	2.7
Other	18.5	3.7	45.9	5.0	22.1	4.0	51.0	5.8
Total	100.0		100.0		100.0	100.2[a]		100.0

SOURCE: U.S. Equal Employment Opportunity Commission, Minorities and Women in State and Local Government, vol. I (Washington, D.C.: U.S. Government Printing Office, 1977), pp. 12-176. Data based upon 2,387 jurisdictions, cited in Robert D. Lee, Jr., Public Personnel Systems (Baltimore: University Park Press, 1979), p. 245; and U.S. Equal Employment Opportunity Commission, "Minorities and Women in State and Local Government, 1985" (Washington, D.C.: U.S. Government Printing Office, 1987).

[a] Varies due to rounding.

local government employees suggests the impact of affirmative action policies and their implementation. Table 6 reveals changes that occurred in the first three years of affirmative action hiring, but the composition of the state and local government workforce was still not representative of the racial and sexual makeup of the general population. The underrepresentation of women and minority groups is illustrated in the "representativeness ratios"[46] contained in Table 6.

The first three years of federally mandated affirmative action programs resulted in an increase from 34.7 percent to 37.4 percent in the female portion of the state and local government workforce. This expansion took place in a time of considerable growth in the workforce in state and local governments. Progress was made by white and black women. Men, however, still held more jobs on the state and local levels than women. Research suggests that the data follow the same pattern of female employment as in the federal workforce. Despite the progress, women are overrepresented in lower-graded positions and occupy a disproportionately small number of high-level positions.[47] The minority workforce in state and local government has fared even worse than women.[48]

Despite changes in the composition of the state and local government workforce during the period from 1975 to 1985, the workforce was still not representative of the racial and sexual makeup of the general population. The underrepresentation of women and some minorities in 1985 is illustrated in the "representativeness ratios" in Table 6. By 1985, white women were represented at only 69 percent of their proportion of the general population, while the figures for Hispanic, Asian, and Indian women were 63 percent, 88 percent, and 67 percent. By contrast, black women were overrepresented as they had been in 1973 and 1975. Among men, the overrepresentation of whites and blacks continued.

In the first twelve years of federally mandated affirmative action programs, female participation in the state and local government workforce increased from 37.4 percent (1973) to 41.1 percent (1985); increases were experienced by white and black women. In contrast, however, men still held more jobs than women in state and local government (58.9 percent in 1985).

Table 6
Minority and Female Representation in State and Local Government Employment, 1973–1985

Group	Percent of General Population 1970	Percent in Bureaucracy 1973	1973 Representativeness Ratio	Percent in Bureaucracy 1975	1975 Representativeness Ratio	Percent of General Population 1980	Percent in Bureaucracy 1985	1980 Representativeness Ratio
White male	40.0	54.7	1.37	51.1	1.28	40.1	45.7	1.14
White female	41.6	27.1	0.65	28.4	0.68	42.8	29.5	0.69
Black male	5.4	7.5	1.39	8.1	1.50	5.5	8.9	1.62
Black female	5.7	6.2	1.09	7.3	1.28	6.2	8.7	1.40
Hispanic male	2.9	2.3	0.79	2.5	0.86	3.2	3.2	1.00
Hispanic female	3.1	1.0	0.32	1.3	0.42	3.2	2.0	0.63
Asian male	0.2	0.3	1.50	0.3	1.50	0.8	0.8	1.00
Asian female	0.2	0.3	1.50	0.3	1.50	0.8	0.7	0.88
Indian male	0.5	0.2	0.40	0.2	0.40	0.3	0.3	1.0
Indian female	0.5	0.1	0.20	0.1	0.20	0.3	0.2	0.67

SOURCE: U.S. Equal Employment Opportunity Commission, Minorities and Women in State and Local Government, 1973, vol. I (Washington, D.C.: U.S. Government Printing Office, 1974); and Equal Employment Opportunity Commission, Minorities and Women in State and Local Government, 1975, vol. I (Washington, D.C.: U.S. Government Printing Office, 1977); cited in N. Joseph Cayer and Lee Sigelman, "Minorities and Women in State and Local Government: 1973–1975," Public Administration Review 40 (September/October 1980): 445; U.S. Equal Employment Opportunity Commission, "Minorities and Women in State and Local Government, 1985" (Washington, D.C.: U.S. Government Printing Office, 1987); and U.S. Department of Commerce, Bureau of the Census, 1980 Census of Population, Characteristics of the Population, vol. 1 (Washington, D.C.: U.S. Government Printing Office, May 1983).

The gains for minorities in the state and local government workforce were even less than for women between 1973 and 1985, with Asian males actually decreasing in their representation.

A recently completed study[49] observes that employment by blacks in city government was at its highest in 1978 and dropped thereafter. In 28 of the 40 cities studied, the number of jobs held by blacks in city government decreased between 1978 and 1980. Blacks, however, did not bear a disproportionate reduction of jobs during this period. In fact, despite the reduction of jobs after 1978, most cities employed more blacks in the city workforce than they did in 1973. Only eleven cities in the survey experienced declines in the number of jobs held by blacks from 1973 to 1980. Cincinnati, Philadelphia, and Rochester (New York) were especially hard hit.[50]

Examination of blacks in city government at the beginning and end of the decade shows their overrepresentation as compared with the total workforce. Between 1970 and 1980, however, black employees lost ground in proportion to the black population as a whole. The black overrepresentation in municipal government can be explained by a high concentration of minority workers in lower-level city jobs. Furthermore, the decline in the population, between 1970 and 1980, of such large cities as Atlanta, Chicago, Cincinnati, Detroit, Milwaukee, New Orleans, Philadelphia, Pittsburgh, St. Louis, and San Francisco can also explain overrepresentation of blacks in municipal government.[51]

Minorities and Women in New York State Government

The ethnic, sex, and salary survey for the New York State government workforce in 1981 comprises data from 75 state agencies (but does not include the State University of New York). A comparison of the composition of government employment in New York State from 1967 to 1981 shows a 37.2 percent increase in the workforce. During the same period minority representation increased by only 6.8 percentage points. Hispanic representation doubled from 1.4 percent of the workforce in 1967 to 2.8 percent of the workforce in 1981.[52]

A comparison of minority and female representation in New York State government employment from 1967 to 1981 reflects an underrepresentation of white females in the current workforce; 48 percent of New York State employees are women. Persons of Hispanic origin are also highly underrepresented in the workforce as compared to the total population.[53]

In the occupational categories in 1981, minorities are best represented (41.7 percent) in the paraprofessional category. Their representation in other occupations is considerably less, with only 14 percent of all professionals in the New York State workforce representing a minority group. More than half of the individuals in each of the paraprofessional and office/clerical occupational categories are women. Their dominance in these occupations, however, is not reflected in the professional category, where only 39.5 percent of the persons in this group are women. This figure is far less than their representation in the general state population.[54]

While summary data may show some advancement in the status of minorities and women in the New York State government workforce, analysis of salary levels and grades reflects the status of these groups more accurately. The following data on public sector employment in New York State illustrate this point:

- Although women make up almost half of the New York State work force, there are almost five men for every woman in the 3,712 top management or public policy making positions. (1981)

- There are also considerable sex differences in salary grade levels. Women constitute 74 percent of all employees in grades 1 to 6. By contrast, men make up 73 percent of all employees in grades 23 and above. (1982)

- White employees outnumber minority employees in the 3,712 top management positions by about nine-to-one, even though minorities are more than one-fifth of the New York State work force. (1981)

- Well over two-thirds (23,912) of all minority employees are below salary grade 14 (entry-level professional), but less than half (63,250) of all white employees are below grade 14. (1982)

- Minorities constitute 35 percent (707) of all employees in grades 31 to 38. However, 74 percent of these employees are Asians or Pacific Islanders in physician titles. If the physician titles are removed, minority employees drop to 13 percent of all employees in those high-level, professional, and managerial grades. (1982)[55]

Thus, the data indicate underrepresentation by minorities and women at significant levels of New York State government.

Minorities and Women in New York City Government

New York City currently employs over 135,000 full-time workers in mayoral agencies. In order to ascertain a profile of representation by minorities and women in the city government workforce and evaluate the impact of current city personnel policies on the minority and female populations, it is important to locate where these jobs are, as well as the salaries they pay.[56]

A comparison of the composition of government employment in New York City from 1975 to 1986 shows approximately the same number of people in the workforce. This reflects a 15 percent increase since 1983 following the fiscal cutbacks. Thirty-two percent (42,720) of the 135,583 full-time New York City mayoral agency employees in 1986 were women. Sixty-nine percent (24,702) in 1983 were minority women. Forty-four percent (59,172) of the city government workforce are members of a minority group. Seventy-five percent of the minority employees are black, 22 percent are Hispanic, and 4 percent of the minority group are Asian or American Indian.

During the period 1975 to 1983, that the city workforce declined, minority representation increased by 10.3 percent. However, minority representation increased in the general city population between 1970 and 1980 by 27.1 percent.[57]

A comparison of minority and female representation in New York City government employment from 1971 to 1983 reflects an underrepresentation of white females in the current workforce. Persons of Hispanic origin, Asians, and American Indians are also highly underrepresented in the workforce, as compared to the total population.[58]

In the occupational categories in 1986, minorities are represented with their largest percentages in the paraprofessions category (80 percent) and the office and clerical category (76 percent). Only 7.7 percent of minorities are in management positions,[59] and only 1.6 percent are skilled craft workers. Women are represented by 80 percent of the positions in the office and clerical category and 50 percent of the paraprofessions category. In 1986, 14.2 percent of women in the city workforce were in management positions.[60] But, in 1981, when 12 percent of women were in these positions, 95 percent of these women occupied one job title: "Principal Administrative Associate," the lowest level managerial title.[61] In 1986, 37 percent of those employed in the professional category were women. This figure is far less than their representation in the general city population.

Minorities and women are concentrated in jobs in certain functional areas. More than 40 percent of the New York City government employees in the areas of financial administration, public welfare, health, housing, and community development were women in 1983. More than half of the jobs in the areas of public welfare and health were held by women. The data further indicate that minorities hold the majority of jobs in the areas of public welfare, health, housing, and corrections. Approximately 35 percent of all jobs held by minorities were in public welfare. Minorities are represented by only approximately 25 percent of the jobs in police protection and sanitation services, and 9.5 percent of the jobs in the functional area of fire protection.[62]

Representation by jobs does not depict fully the status of minorities and women in the city workforce. An analysis of minorities and women by salary distribution in 1981 illustrates that these groups do not fare as well in the city workforce as their numbers might indicate.[63]

In analyzing the distribution of minorities in the New York City workforce, it is worthy of note to examine the teaching staff in relation to the ethnic composition of the student body. This review is particularly important because

on November 9, 1976, the Office of Civil Rights issued a letter of findings which concluded that the Board of Education had engaged in discriminatory practices under Title VI and Title IX with respect to the hiring and assigning of minority faculty and the appointment of women supervisory personnel.[64]

The most dramatic evidence to be uncovered by the Office of Civil Rights was that other large cities seemed to do better in the hiring of minorities in the schools, despite certain conditions over which school boards have no control. New York City's "ratio of minority-group teachers to minority students was the lowest of all major cities."[65]

Conclusions

Stress exists in the system between the notion of equity and the implementation of standard requirements for selection. While civil service portends to be an open system, it excludes those with disadvantaged educational and social backgrounds from competing on an equal basis.[66]

For the most part minorities and women have been at a competitive disadvantage in public employment in the United States. The data indicate that while minorities and women maintain a share of jobs in the government workforce, they have not fared well in obtaining the high-ranking, better paying jobs within the bureaucracy.[67]

It is worthy of note that of all levels of government, city government bureaucracies were found to be the most representative. Minorities are better represented in local government employment than some would have assumed. Women, however, are probably less represented than many would have believed.

Despite the success which minorities have experienced in obtaining civil service jobs, they have not done as well at attaining higher occupational level jobs. For those minorities who do attain these positions, they are not as successful at achieving comparable wages as nonminorities are for their work. The same would hold true for women as compared to men.

In reviewing the hypothesis of this study that the rigid structure of municipal civil service systems and the principle of meritocracy underlying that system have maintained a system of social inequity, it is worth noting here that, while attempts are often made through recruitment procedures to hire minorities in the city workforce, devices in the civil service system dealing with salaries and promotional opportunities are not as favorable for minorities and women.[68]

ISSUES ASSOCIATED WITH AFFIRMATIVE ACTION

There are several issues associated with efforts to achieve affirmative action which have had an impact on these efforts. Such issues include quotas and "reverse discrimination," fiscal cutbacks and seniority, and veterans' preference.

Quotas and "Reverse Discrimination"

This issue relates to the debate concerning the mechanism for increasing the number of minority group members and women in the public service. It has been suggested by some that efforts to eliminate the barriers on hiring strengthen merit systems, but that the use of preferential hiring and quota systems is detrimental to the concept of employing persons by merit.[69] Still others debate that the use of preferential hiring is critical in compensating for discriminatory hiring practices of the past. Many holding this position also believe that civil service examinations, procedures, laws, and standards discriminate against minority groups because they represent a middle-class value system characterized by educational levels and culture of the middle class, and that they need to be restructured.[70]

The difference between goals and quotas as they relate to the hiring of minorities and women is that goals generally refer to targets or objectives for hiring a specified percentage of minorities or women within a period of time while quotas, in contrast, mandate requirements for hiring based upon race, sex, or ethnicity. Those who are in favor of quotas believe that no real change will occur without the required use of quotas. They also contend that many job seekers have been precluded from obtaining government jobs due to the use of the merit system.[71]

It is relevant to recall that when the patronage system flourished, ethnic minority groups obtained jobs by promising their vote to the political party. In contrast to the civil service examination system of today, entrance into the patronage system was easier. Today, minorities who score comparatively low on the civil service examination have little chance of obtaining employment in the government workforce. This is despite the fact that these minority groups may comprise the majority of the electorate in an election district.[72]

Arguments for goals in contrast to quotas are based on the notions of equality and merit. Those opposed to quotas suggest that "quotas are antithetical to equality," because they deny jobs to some and not to others. It is suggested that this is reverse discrimination and is in violation of equal protection of the laws guaranteed in the Fourteenth Amendment. Moreover, quotas are alleged to be contradictory to merit since less competent workers may be hired when more competent ones are available as a result of the process.[73]

The establishment of both goals and quotas is used today. While goals are most common, the courts have imposed quotas on various government agencies to remedy racial and sexual imbalances. The federal courts, for example, have required the use of quotas in certain local fire departments and state and local police departments. In some instances, quotas established by various officials are the subject of legal action as allegedly constituting reverse discrimination.[74]

It is only recently that the United States Supreme Court has addressed the issue of quotas in government employment. The Court previously examined the use of quotas in college admissions procedures. In the case of *Regents of the University of California v. Bakke*,[75] the Court examined whether whites were discriminated against with regard to quotas established for admitting minority students to the University of California at Davis Medical School. While the Court ruled that a quota system was a form of reverse discrimination, it did agree that race can be made a factor in admitting minorities. It is against this background that government employment cases were later decided.[76]

In two separate decisions on July 2, 1986, the Supreme Court rejected the Reagan administration's policies and arguments which it had been attempting to promote in civil rights. The Justice Department had argued that the use of numerical goals in hiring and promotion for those not individually identified as victims of discrimination violates the Constitution. The Court rejected that argument in cases pertaining to the Cleveland Fire Department and a New York labor union.[77]

In *Firefighters v. Cleveland*[78] the Court held that lower federal courts have the authority to mandate preferential hiring or promotion of minority group members who are not personally victims of discrimination as a remedy for past discrimination. In the case of *Sheet Metal Workers v. EEOC*[79] the Court decided that judges may order preferential treatment for minority group members in union membership in order to remedy especially "egregious" discrimination.

In a case involving the Alabama state police department, the Supreme Court, in a highly divided decision, again rejecting the Reagan administration position, recently ruled in *United States v. Paradise*[80] that courts, in extreme cases, could mandate racial preferential hiring and promotion. For the first time, however, the Court specified that numerical quotas could be used to bring a workforce into line as to be representative of the percentage of minority groups in the availability pool.

On March 25, 1987, the Supreme Court for the first time entered a decision involving an affirmative action plan giving hiring preference to women over men. In the case of *Johnson v. Transportation Agency*,[81] the Court ruled 6–3 that an employer may give preference to women and minority members over better qualified men and whites in the hiring and promotion process in order to achieve a more representative balance in the workforce. The ruling upheld a California city affirmative action plan, and further struck down the Reagan administration efforts to assault affirmative action.

Acceptance of the theory of "reverse discrimination" by judicial or executive branches of government would thwart advances in affirmative action. One can rationalize that if a discriminatory appointments policy is adopted to relieve a social wrong, and it favors a disadvantaged group, then the discriminatory policy is not necessarily unjust even if this results in deviating from a meritocratic system.[82]

Fiscal Cutbacks and Seniority

As a result of the fiscal crisis faced by many municipalities in the 1970s, and still others in the 1980s, new terminology has entered the field of public administration. Such terms as "fiscal cutbacks," "cutback management," and "last hired, first fired" are among those which will continue to be prevalent in the 1980s. This phenomenon of fiscal cutbacks as it relates to seniority systems within government agencies has had its impact on affirmative action programs.

A survey projected that 15,000 federal layoffs were forecasted by the end of 1982. Record numbers of layoffs in government workforces were expected at the state and local levels as well.[83]

In determining whether civil service positions are eliminated in good faith, the courts have applied two basic rules: (1) "the abolition of a civil service position must not be a subterfuge to remove the individual, while leaving the position intact," and (2) "on whether the abolished position was truly abolished or whether it remained in existence under a different name."[84] Thus, the courts have focused particularly on evidence demonstrating how economic interests were served by the elimination of positions.

While municipal staff reductions may have been eliminated in "good faith," they have, in fact, had an impact on many municipal affirmative action programs. Dominating the working careers of minorities and women has been the impact of the principle of last hired and first fired, which is characterized by a rigid seniority system. This principle is an integral part of civil service systems as well as union contracts. Since minorities and women are the last hired and have the least seniority they are most likely to be subject to any reductions.[85] The last twenty years of legislation and judicial decisions have had an impact on the ability of last hired minorities to survive future cutbacks.[86]

Those minorities and women who entered the public sector as a result of increased employment opportunities and affirmative action programs were severely impacted by the 1974–1975 recession. Of particular severity was the financial crisis that hit New York City, which forced the city to lay off thousands of workers during the spring and summer of 1975. Some 2,500 police officers were fired as part of these layoffs. Since the New York Civil Service Law mandates that employees hired last be laid off first in case of staff cutbacks, the layoffs had a severe impact on minority and women police officers in the New York City Police Department. Data indicate that as a result of the cutbacks women police officers were cut by 73.5 percent. Male police officers were reduced by only 23.9 percent. A high percentage of the males laid off were black or Hispanic.[87]

Women and minority police officers subsequently litigated to block the layoffs (*Acha v. Beame*, 1975). On appeal, the United States Court of Appeals for the Second Circuit reversed the ruling of the United States District Court with regard to awarding retroactive seniority (*Acha v. Beame*, 1976).[88]

The Court of Appeals proceeded to outline the rule that would apply in determining retroactive seniority, and the ruling required the retrenched police officer to demonstrate that she tried to get a job or had shown interest in a position with the police department prior to awarding of retroactive seniority.[89] Shortly after this ruling the Supreme Court ruled that the federal courts could award retroactive seniority under certain circumstances (*Franks v. Bowman Transportation Company*, 1976). It is important to remember, however, that as a result of the rulings in the *Franks* and *International Brotherhood of Teamsters v. United States* (1977) cases, permitting bona fide seniority systems, it appears that the municipalities have little flexibility in saving the "last hired."[90]

In recent rulings the Supreme Court supported the notion of seniority. The Court decided in 1984 that the Civil Rights Act prevented a federal judge from mandating that black firefighters in Memphis with less seniority keep their jobs while white firefighters with greater seniority were laid off (*Firefighters Local Union No. 1784 v. Stotts*, 1984).[91] In 1986, the Court struck down a plan by the Jackson, Michigan, school board for laying off white teachers before minority group teachers. A majority of the justices did, however, say that governments could be permitted to give preferential treatment to minorities in the hiring process to remedy past discrimination, but not in layoffs (*Wygant v. Jackson Bd. of Educ.*, 1986).[92]

There are, however, other alternatives which can be structured to avoid the inevitable adverse affects on minorities and women. In Detroit, for example, residents have been willing to increase taxes, unions agreed to wage concessions, and there has been discussion about decreasing nonwage items (e.g., personal days, break time, vacation times and schedules) as alternatives to the next round of layoffs.[93]

In New York City in 1975, the municipal unions proposed a

similar plan including relinquishing some personal leave time, cutting overtime, and waiving the city's share of the union's health and welfare fund, while setting a two-month waiting period before new workers could be eligible for such benefits.[94]

It has been suggested that fiscal cutbacks are the vulnerable component of the personnel system. As such it is open to political manipulation. In order to protect any accomplishments achieved by affirmative action programs, it is essential for personnel professionals to promote the notion of equity in fiscal cutbacks. Minorities and women will need much support in fighting the seniority system. Affirmative action gains are essential if civil service systems are to attain the goal of social equity.[95]

Veterans' Preference

As a reward for their service in the military, veterans have long been the beneficiaries of preferential treatment in civil service employment. Most localities, most states, and the federal government award an initial hiring preference to veterans who pass the civil service tests. These are usually in the form of a point preference or a tie-breaking preference. This system provides veterans with a competitive advantage over eligible nonveterans.[96] In contrast, however, it places women competing for the same jobs at a clear disadvantage.

In a case dealing with the veterans' preference issue in Massachusetts, a woman alleged that the "absolute preference formula operated to systematically exclude eligible women from consideration for upper-level civil service positions."[97] She claimed that this was in violation of both the equal protection and due process clauses of the Fourteenth Amendment. In Massachusetts the preference is *permanent*, in that it can be used indefinitely, and *absolute*, in that it places veterans ahead of nonveterans regardless of their examination scores.[98]

The U.S. District Court ignored the Massachusetts statute's continuation of gender discrimination. In doing so it required the plaintiff to prove that the Massachusetts legislature enacted the absolute veterans' preference specifically to discriminate against women. The court ruled that "the 14th Amendment guarantees equal laws, not equal results, and held that the racially disparate impact of a facially neutral law must be traced to an underlying discriminatory purpose."[99] The Supreme Court upheld the decision.

In another case, the Montana Supreme Court recently ruled that the state had been misinterpreting the laws written in the 1920s giving preference to veterans. The court ruled that: "Instead of using veterans' preference as a tie-breaker when two candidates are equally qualified, veterans should have preference for any job they apply for and for which they are minimally qualified."[100]

Needless to say this has caused much furor in Montana. Women's groups and legislators are seeking to make changes in the law while veterans' groups vehemently oppose any restructuring of the law. In the interim the state personnel director indicated that more than 90 percent of the positions available the first six months that the court handed down its ruling went to veterans.[101]

A recent study concerning the impact of organizational constraints on municipal affirmative action concludes that some cities have their affirmative action efforts constrained by certain organizational characteristics. It is suggested that affirmative action strategies for increased female employment representation are most likely to develop in cities with the fewest organizational constraints, while cities with organizational barriers will most probably retain veterans' preference systems that impede social equity.[102] These conditions highlight the complexity of efforts to achieve affirmative action. The success of these programs will depend upon balancing and sorting out these complex factors.

CONCLUSIONS

This chapter demonstrates that employment opportunities for minorities and women have not been achieved through passive programs. As a result of allegations of discrimination by reformers in the 1960s, affirmative action programs were developed in an attempt to achieve improvements for minority groups and women in public jobs. Some civil service professionals supporting these programs interpreted such efforts as advertising job openings and tests and eliminating inappropriate job requirements as positive. They were in favor of affirmative action on a theoretical basis, just as long as attempts at achieving social equity did not interfere with their long-cherished traditional principles of merit. Modifications in the system were accepted only to improve efficiency, not for purposes of eliminating the barriers which maintain inequities.[103]

In evaluating achievements of affirmative action programs, it is important to examine how bias may be a factor in personnel selection, despite apparent safeguards. A study of the selection of middle- and senior-level managers in Los Angeles County government indicated from available evidence that affirmative action requirements do not balance out the effects of bias.[104]

These examples illustrate the difficulty in achieving affirmative action. Major barriers to the implementation of affirmative action in municipal civil service systems continue to exist. Racist and sexist attitudes by those officials responsible for maintaining the system, union pressure to maintain seniority systems, belief that affirmative action is synonymous with reverse discrimination, and insistance by personnel administrators in maintaining strong merit principles regardless of their impact on social equity, all contribute to the difficulty of implementing affirmative action in municipal civil service systems. Despite these considerable barriers, some progress is being made. It is important for research to examine this progress over time.[105] One of the objectives of this study is to make a contribution to this needed research.

NOTES

1. Don Hellriegel and Larry Short, "Equal Employment Opportunity in the Federal Government: A Comparative Analysis," *Public Administration Review* 32 (November/December 1972): 851–857.

2. Frederick C. Mosher, *Democracy and the Public Service* (New York: Oxford University Press, 1968), p. 208.

3. Hellriegel and Short, "Equal Employment Opportunity in the Federal Government," pp. 851–857.

4. Grace Hall Saltzstein, "Institutional Barriers to Representativeness in Bureaucracy: The Residual Effects of Organizational Reform,"

paper presented at the Annual Conference of the American Society for Public Administration, New York, 16–19 April 1983, p. 5.

5. Catherine Lovell, "Three Keys in Affirmative Action," *Public Administration Review* 34 (May/June 1974): 235.

6. The work of Nathan Glazer depicts the opposition surrounding affirmative action programs; Nathan Glazer, *Affirmative Discrimination: Ethnic Inequality and Public Policy* (New York: Basic Books, 1975), pp. 196–197, 221.

7. "U.S. Easing Rules on Discrimination by Its Contractors," *New York Times*, 25 August 1981, sec. 1, p. 1.

8. "Breaking New Ground on Affirmative Action," *New York Times*, 21 May 1986, sec. A, p. 28; and "Number of Blacks in Top Jobs in Administration Off Sharply," *New York Times*, 22 March 1987, sec. A, p. 1.

9. Lloyd G. Nigro, "Some Concluding Observations," *Public Administration Review* 34 (May/June 1974): 246.

10. Robert D. Lee, Jr., *Public Personnel Systems* (Baltimore: University Park Press, 1979), p. 248.

11. Georgetown University, *What Achieves Affirmative Action in Cities?* (Washington, D.C.: Public Services Laboratory, Georgetown University, 1975), p. 5.

12. Ibid., pp. 5–6.

13. James C. Renick, "The Impact of Municipal Affirmative Action Programs on Black Representation in Government Employment: Reality or Rhetoric?" *Southern Review of Public Administration* 5 (Summer 1981): 129.

14. Lee, *Public Personnel Systems*, p. 248.

15. Ibid., p. 271.

16. Ibid., p. 272.

17. Ibid.

18. Frank J. Thompson, "Meritocracy, Equality and Employment: Commitment to Minority Hiring Among Public Officials," paper presented at the 1976 Annual Meeting of the American Political Science Association, Chicago, 2–5 September 1976, pp. 2–3.

19. Ibid., p. 3.

20. Ibid., p. 4.

21. Ibid.

22. Ibid., pp. 5–6.

23. Ibid., p. 9.

24. Ibid., p. 14.

25. Ibid., p. 17. Similar conclusions were obtained in a study of city managers with regard to their commitment to affirmative action; see

James D. Slack, "Affirmative Action and City Managers: Attitudes Toward Recruitment of Women," *Public Administration Review* 47 (March/April 1987): 199–206.

26. It is worth noting that a study of the impact of tutoring minorities for police officer positions concluded that test scores for minorities increased, diminishing the discriminatory impact on hiring. Robert Panzarella, "The Impact of Tutoring Minority Recruits for Civil Service Exams for Police Officer Selection," *Review of Public Personnel Administration* 6 (Spring 1986): 59–71.

27. Frank J. Thompson, *Personnel Policy in the City: The Politics of Jobs in Oakland* (Berkeley, Calif.: University of California Press, 1975), pp. 136–137.

28. Interview with Supervisor of Office Supplies, Environmental Protection Agency, City of New York, 15 August 1973.

29. Sylvia Drew Ivie, "Discrimination in Selection and Promotion of Minorities and Women in Municipal Employment," *The Urban Lawyer* 7 (Summer 1975): 540.

30. Thompson, "Meritocracy, Equality and Employment," p. 15.

31. Thomas Sowell, "Affirmative Action Harms the Disadvantaged," *Wall Street Journal*, 28 July 1981, p. 28.

32. Renick, "The Impact of Municipal Affirmative Action Programs on Black Representation in Government Employment," p. 130.

33. Ibid.

34. Joseph P. Viteritti, *Bureaucracy and Social Justice: The Allocation of Jobs and Services to Minority Groups* (Port Washington, N.Y.: Kennikat Press, 1979), pp. 91–92.

35. In 1975, Kenneth Meier reported similar findings in his research; ibid., p. 92.

36. Ibid.

37. Ibid., p. 93.

38. Lee, *Public Personnel Systems*, p. 243.

39. Winfield H. Rose and Tiang Ping Chia, "The Impact of the Equal Employment Opportunity Act of 1972 on Black Employment in the Federal Service: A Preliminary Analysis," *Public Administration Review* 38 (May/June 1978): 251.

40. Lee, *Public Personnel Systems*, p. 244.

41. U.S. Equal Employment Opportunity Commission, *Job Patterns for Minorities and Women in State and Local Government, 1980* (Washington, D.C.: U.S. Government Printing Office, 1982), p. ix.

42. Lee, *Public Personnel Systems*, pp. 244–245.

43. Ibid., pp. 245–246.

44. Ibid., p. 246.

45. Edward B. Fiske, "Enrollment of Minorities in Colleges Stagnating," *New York Times*, 19 April 1987, sec. A, p. 1.

46. N. Joseph Cayer and Lee Sigelman calculated the representativeness ratios by dividing each group's percentage of government jobs by the percentage each group comprises of the general population. Thus, a ratio of 1.0 means that a group occupied the same proportion of government jobs that it did of the general population; a lower ratio signifies numerical underrepresentation, and a higher ratio overrepresentation.

47. N. Joseph Cayer and Lee Sigelman, "Minorities and Women in State and Local Government: 1973–1975," *Public Administration Review* 40 (September/October 1980): 449.

48. Ibid., p. 450.

49. Peter K. Eisinger, *Black Employment in City Government, 1973–1980* (Washington, D.C.: Joint Center for Political Studies, 1983); while New York City was not included in Eisinger's study, it also experienced severe cuts.

50. Ibid., pp. 6–8.

51. Ibid., pp. 9, 52.

52. New York State Department of Civil Service, *Report on the Ethnic Survey of the Work Force of New York State Agencies, 1979–1980–1981* (Albany, N.Y.: New York State Department of Civil Service, n.d.), p. 13.

53. Ibid.

54. Ibid., and Lillie McLaughlin, *Detailed Statistics on Women and Minorities in New York State and New York City Government Employment: 1981–82* (Albany, N.Y.: Center for Women in Government, State University of New York at Albany, Spring 1983).

55. McLaughlin, *Detailed Statistics on Women and Minorities in New York State*, p. 1; and "Statement by City Personnel Director Judith A. Levitt on Minority Representation in the Workforce Before the City Council's Civil Service and Labor Committee," 11 March 1987.

56. Government workforce data on New York City were obtained from the New York City Human Rights Commission, the New York City Department of Personnel, and reports from the Center for Women in Government. Data for 1975 and 1986 reflect employees in mayoral agencies and do not include nonmayoral agency employees of the Board of Education or the Health and Hospitals Corporation, both large employers. It is important to note that, in order to obtain some earlier data from 1983 on the New York City government workforce, it was necessary to write to the Human Rights Commission and the Department of Personnel and make the request under the Freedom of Information Act. Such information is not readily available to the public. One 1982

summary table by occupation is available in the Human Rights Commission's *Annual Report*. This, however, compares quite poorly to the availability of printed affirmative action data in government workforces by the federal government and New York State. Review of the data in the City Department of Personnel indicates that the data are prepared in standardized EEO–4 format as required for submission to the federal government. The status of these data, particularly salary data, is in raw form and requires long hours to create summary tables. Summary tables, however, are published for federal and New York State data.

In attempting to obtain the data through several officials, especially in the Department of Personnel, it became clear that a policy exists in city government not to make racial and sexual city workforce data easily accessible to the public. I was told that certain summary tables were made available to the mayor, but that I would be required to file a subpoena in order to obtain them. It would appear that the leadership is lacking to make the system open, insofar as these data are maintained within the agencies.

57. New York City Commission on Human Rights, *The Employment of Minorities, Women and the Handicapped in City Government: A Report of a 1971 Survey*, September 1973; New York Cty Commission on Human Rights, *Cumulative Workforce Analysis by EEO Category*, 30 June 1975 and 30 June 1983; and U.S. Department of Commerce, Bureau of the Census, *1980 Census of Population. Characteristics of Inhabitants. New York, vol. 1, Characteristics of the Population* (Washington, D.C.: U.S. Government Printing Office, February 1982), pp. 34–105.

58. New York City Commission on Human Rights, *The Employment of Minorities, Women and the Handicapped in City Government*; New York City Commission on Human Rights, *Cumulative Workforce Analysis by EEO Category*; and U.S. Department of Commerce, Bureau of the Census, *1980 Census of Population*.

59. "Federal Equal Employment Opportunity Commission Survey Form (EEO–4) Occupational Category: Officials and Administrators—occupations in which employees set broad policies, exercise overall responsibility for execution of these policies, or direct individual departments or special phases of the agency's operation or provide specialized consultation on a regional, district, or area basis." Noted in McLaughlin, *Detailed Statistics on Women and Minorities in New York State and New York City Government Employment*, p. 6.

60. "Statement by City Personnel Director."

61. McLaughlin, *Detailed Statistics on Women and Minorities in New York State and New York City Government Employment*, p. 6.

62. New York City, Department of Personnel, *EEOC Local Government Information Report (EEO–4) City of New York*, 30 June 1983.

63. McLaughlin, *Detailed Statistics on Women and Minorities in New York State and New York City Government Employment*, pp. 6–7. See also NYU Urban Research Center, *Wage Discrimination and Occupational Segregation in New York City's Municipal Work Force: Time for a Change* (New York: Urban Research Center, New York University Graduate School of Public Administration, August 1987) for the results of a study that highlights occupational segregation and wage discrimination for females and minorities in the New York City municipal work force.

64. Interface, "The Effects of Selected Urban Policies on Equal Opportunity in New York City," draft study sponsored by the New York State Advisory Committee for the U.S. Commission on Civil Rights, May 1981, sec. I, p. 42. (Mimeographed paper.) The views expressed are those of Interface staff and should not be attributed to the Commissioners.

65. "New York City Reflected in Its Schools," *New York Times*, 14 November 1976.

66. Viteritti, *Bureaucracy and Social Justice*, pp. 107–108.

67. Ibid., p. 108.

68. Ibid., p. 109.

69. Georgetown University, *What Achieves Affirmative Action in Cities?* p. 7.

70. Ibid., p. 8.

71. Lee, *Public Personnel Systems*, pp. 274–275.

72. Ibid., p. 275.

73. Ibid.

74. Lee, *Public Personnel Systems*, p. 276.

75. *Regents of the University of California v. Bakke*, 98 S. Ct. 2733 (1978). For the debate surrounding "reverse discrimination" versus affirmative action in academia see also *Defunis v. Odegaard*, 82 Wash. 2d 11, 507 P. 2d 1169, cert. granted, 414 U.S. 1038 (1973).

76. Lee, *Public Personnel Systems*, p. 277.

77. "Affirmative Action Upheld by High Court as a Remedy for Past Job Discrimination," *New York Times*, 3 July 1986, sec. A, p. 1.

78. *Firefighters v. Cleveland*, 106 S. Ct. 3063 (1986).

79. *Sheet Metal Workers v. EEOC*, 106 S. Ct. 3019 (1986).

80. *United States v. Paradise*, 107 S. Ct. 1053 (1987).

81. *Johnson v. Transportation Agency*, 480 U.S. _____, 94 L Ed 2d 615 (1987).

82. Thomas Nagel, "Equal Treatment and Compensatory Discrimination," in *Equality and Preferential Treatment*, eds. Marshall Cohen, Thomas Nagel, and Thomas Scanlon (Princeton, N.J.: Princeton University Press, 1977), p. 17.

83. Edward J. Williams and James R. Macy, "Municipal Staff Reductions," *Wisconsin Bar Bulletin* 56 (February 1983): 13.

84. James O. Pearson, Jr., "Determination as to Good Faith in Abolition of Public Office or Employment Subject to Civil Service or Merit System," 87 ALR 3d 1165 (1978).

85. Wilbur C. Rich, "Bumping, Blocking and Bargaining: The Effect of Layoffs on Employees and Unions," *Review of Public Personnel Administration* 4 (Fall 1983): 40.

86. For a discussion of the cases related to seniority systems see Marcia Graham, "Seniority Systems and Title VII—Reanalysis and Redirection," *Employee Relations Law Journal* 9 (Summer 1983): 81–97; Thomas R. Bagby, "The Supreme Court Reaffirms Broad Immunity for Seniority Systems," *Labor Law Journal* 33 (July 1982): 409–416; and Robert N. Roberts, "'Last Hired, First Fired' and Public Employee Layoffs: The Equal Employment Opportunity Dilemma," *Review of Public Personnel Administration* 2 (Fall 1981): 29–48.

87. Roberts, "'Last Hired, First Fired' and Public Employee Layoffs," p. 31.

88. Ibid., p. 35.

89. Ibid.

90. Ibid.; for further discussion of retroactive seniority see Hindy Lauer Schachter, "Retroactive Seniority and Agency Retrenchment," *Public Administration Review* 43 (January/February 1983): 77–81; Linda Greenhouse, "Seniority Is Held to Outweigh Race as a Layoff Guide," *New York Times*, 13 June 1984, pp. Al, Bll.

91. *Firefighters Local Union No. 1784 v. Stotts*, 467 U.S. 561 (1984).

92. *Wygant v. Jackson Bd. of Educ.*, 106 S. Ct. 1842 (1986).

93. Rich, "Bumping, Blocking and Bargaining," p. 41.

94. "Head of Equal Employment Unit Said to Plan Layoff Guidelines," *New York Times*, 3 February 1975.

95. Rich, "Bumping, Blocking and Bargaining," p. 42.

96. Constance A. Browne, "Absolute Veterans' Preference in Public Employment: Personnel Administrator of Massachusetts v. Feeney," *Boston College Law Review* 21 (July 1980): 1110.

97. Ibid., p. 1113.

98. Ibid., p. 1111.

99. Ibid., p. 1141.

100. "Montana Debates Law on Hiring Veterans," *New York Times*, 13 November 1983, p. 65.

101. Ibid.

102. Grace Hall Saltzstein, "External Pressures, Organizational Constraints, and Change: The Case of Municipal Affirmative Action," paper

presented at the Annual Meeting of the American Political Science Association, Chicago, 1–4 September 1983, p. 15.

103. Mosher, *Democracy and the Public Service*, 2nd ed., pp. 224–225.

104. Mike Jackson, "Racial Factors in Executive Selection," *Public Personnel Management* 8 (July/August 1979): 221.

105. Mitchell F. Rice and George Johnson, "Affirmative Action and Equal Employment Opportunity in a Municipal Government: A Preliminary Analysis and Case Study of San Antonio, Texas—1974 to 1979," draft paper prepared for delivery at the Annual Conference of the American Society for Public Administration, Detroit, 12–15 April 1981, p. 7.

Challenges to the Merit System: Litigation Aimed at Eliminating Discriminatory Aspects of Civil Service Systems

4

As in other important areas of efforts to attain social justice in America, the courts have been an important source of social and institutional change in civil service systems. In the 1960s, concerns about civil service began to emerge as a result of pressures to make existing institutions more representative and equitable; increasing civil service jobs for minorities was an important goal. New goals set by Community Action Programs (CAP), Model Cities programs, and other community-based organizations served as a catalyst for a more comprehensive evaluation of civil service personnel policies and procedures and why they were exclusionary. A series of legal actions based upon civil rights legislation and the U.S. Constitution began to focus on these issues.[1]

This chapter will examine several cases challenging civil service examination procedures and selection procedures on the ground that they violate the Constitution and/or Title VII of the Civil Rights Act of 1964, in that they discriminate against minority groups and women and are not based on merit because they fail to be "job-related." Ironically, however, the first major case in this area involved a private company. The decision of the Supreme Court in *Griggs v. Duke Power Company*,[2] however, was to set a precedent for all future cases involving private and public employment testing and selection practices that resulted in the exclusion of disproportionate numbers of minority group members. Other selected cases to be included in this analysis focus on the public sector and the selection of principals and other supervisory personnel in the New York City school system, the hiring of entry-level police officers and the promotion of sergeants in the New York City Police Department, and the selection of firefighters in the New York City Fire Department.

Given the role that the courts have played in the American system, as key actors especially in the area of rights, it is necessary to examine what results were achieved through judicial action to change the status of minorities and women in civil service systems. It is also important to determine if change occurred as a result of threatened legal sanctions. Assuming the underlying premise of this study that the rigid structure of municipal civil service systems and the principle of meritocracy underlying that system have contributed to and maintained a system of social inequity, is it possible to change the system through legal action despite these structural barriers?

Beginning in the 1970s and continuing in the 1980s, a series of legal actions by plaintiffs, especially class-action suits, were brought as a response to the reluctance by the legislative and executive branches of government to abolish discriminatory aspects of municipal civil service systems. Many of these groups considered the courts to be a last resort.

Many of the court decisions in these class-action suits contain remedial decrees. In contrast to the final decrees of traditional litigation, which require that the defendant take a specific action, the remedial decree frequently involves the court in an extensive oversight capacity to implement new policies and practices mandated to remedy the problems raised by the case.[3]

LAW AND LEGISLATION PROHIBITING DISCRIMINATION IN PUBLIC EMPLOYMENT

The Fifth and Fourteenth Amendments to the Constitution are the basis for prohibiting discriminatory practices in employment in federal, state, and local governments. (The Fifth Amendment states that "No person shall . . . be deprived of life, liberty, or property, without due process of law." The Fourteenth Amendment states that "No state shall . . . deny to any person within its jurisdiction the equal protection of the laws.") Governments are also prohibited from discriminating in employment by statutory provisions, administrative regulations, and contractual agreements.[4] This general constitutional prohibition is supported by a series of important administrative regulations. On the federal level, Executive Order 11246 (1965), as amended by Executive Order 11375 (1967), prohibits employment discrimination by employers with federal contracts of more than $10,000. Executive Order 11375 had expanded the coverage of Order 11246 to include prohibition against sex discrimination.

Most state constitutions have provisions patterned after the Fifth and Fourteenth Amendments which prohibit discrimination in employment in all state and local governments. State and local governments are also prohibited by the Civil Rights Act of 1871, 42 U.S.C. § 1983, from instituting any state customs or regulations which have a discriminatory effect.[5] It should be noted, however, that despite these numerous provisions the question of what does and does not constitute discrimination is the basis of much controversy in the courts.

Title VII of the Civil Rights Act of 1964 was a landmark in the move to combat discrimination. With the passage of the Equal Employment Opportunity Act of 1972, Congress expanded Title VII to include academic institutions and public as well as private employment.[6] Nearly all states and local governments have enacted employment discrimination legislation patterned after Title VII. Title VII "proscribes not only overt or explicit discrimination . . . but also prohibits practices that are fair in form but discriminatory in operation."[7]

In cases involving discriminatory employment practices, the courts have accepted varied evidence including statistics, discriminatory application of standards, past discrimination, subjective decision making, and discrimination on an individual basis. Moreover, the courts have held that they have the power to grant relief in cases of employment discrimination. Specific forms of relief utilized by the courts to end ongoing discrimination include immediate hire or work referral, recruitment and advertising directed to minorities and women, imposition of numerical remedies and ratios to ensure participation of minorities and women in employment opportunities, restructuring of seniority systems, work referral and testing practices, and monetary awards including back pay.;8

GRIGGS V. DUKE POWER COMPANY

The precedent-setting case dealing with examination and job requirements is *Griggs v. Duke Power Company*, in which the Supreme Court "ruled that job applicants must be evaluated on the basis of skills related to job performance and not on the basis of credentials; it questioned credential requirements as a meaningful basis for hiring."[9] The Court stated that Title VII of the Civil Rights Act of 1964 mandated that the burden of proof demonstrating the relevancy of job requirements to employment rests with the employer.

The *Griggs* action was brought by black employees of the Duke Power Company against their employer in the United States District Court for the Middle District of North Carolina. These employees alleged that the employer violated the Civil Rights Act of 1964 when the company instituted new testing procedures for movement within the company. The new requirements were a high school diploma and satisfactory performance on the Wonderlic Personnel Test and the Bennett Mechanical Aptitude Test for particular jobs previously limited to white employees. The District Court dismissed the complaint.[10] The United States Court of Appeals for the Fourth Circuit reversed the District Court's decision that residual discrimination arising from previous employment procedures was insulated from remedial action, but it affirmed the District Court's ruling that without discriminatory intent, the diploma and test requirements were proper.[11]

On certiorari, the U.S. Supreme Court reversed the Court of Appeals. In a unanimous opinion, the Court held:

that the Civil Rights Act prohibits an employer from requiring a high school education or passing of a standardized general intelligence test as a condition of employment in or transfer to jobs when (1) neither standard is shown to be significantly related to successful job performance, (2) both requirements operate to disqualify Negroes at a substantially higher rate than white applicants, and (3) the jobs in question formerly had been filled only by white employees as part of a long-standing practice of giving preference to whites.[12]

In shaping its decision in *Griggs v. Duke Power Company*, the Court established precedent in two areas. First, in using the Equal Employment Opportunity Commission's Guidelines on Employment Testing Procedures, the Court followed the intent of Congress. EEOC guidelines assume a test to be unlawful unless it has been validated, it demonstrates a significant degree of utility, and other procedures are not available at the time.[13]

Second, the Court adopted several principles concerning employment selection devices. It ruled:

- that employment selection devices, although neutral on their face, are unlawful if they operate to freeze the status quo or to perpetuate the effects of past discrimination;
- that it is not necessary to prove that the defendants intended to discriminate;
- that the burden is on the defendants to show that any given requirement for employment is specifically related to job performance.[14]

Numerous employment discrimination cases over the past fifteen years have served to expose the allocation process of jobs to a variety of groups in society. The litigation has highlighted the myth that most jobs are allocated through meritocratic principle. Selection practices were not criticized because they failed to meet validation standards, but rather because the courts found them to be inconsistent with merit selection. Because it was difficult to rationalize the employment selection practices in meritocratic terms, the courts increased their willingness to apply strict validation standards.[15]

It is important, in terms of the application of *Griggs*, to focus on the central rationale of the Supreme Court's decision. The Supreme Court assumed equality among different races in terms of ability and intelligence. They questioned the utility of traditional employment selection devices. This rationale has provided the basis for attempts at implementing affirmative action programs, a rationale more palitable to program recipients than the concept of "preferential treatment."[16]

The significance of the Supreme Court's decision in *Griggs v. Duke Power Company* on public employment even though it was a private case, and the impact of the principles developed in the case, can be observed in the civil service cases related to discriminatory selection.

CHANCE V. BOARD OF EXAMINERS

In order to comprehend the significance of *Chance v. Board of Examiners*[17] it is important to examine the historical setting of the case. This case challenged the selection procedures for principals and other supervisory personnel in the New York City school system on the ground that the procedures were discriminatory.[18]

Boston Chance, a black, and Louis Mercado, a Puerto Rican, were "acting principals" in the elementary schools in New York City in the fall of 1970. Both had been appointed to their positions by their local community school boards. While both held the credentials and experience required for state certification as principals, in order to be permanently appointed in New York City, they had to be certified based on their performance on a competitive examination administered by the Board of Examiners. Chance had failed the written part of the examination and Mercado refused to take it because he believed it to be discriminatory. Due to the fact that their appointments were made during an interim period between the completion of an old promotion list and the promulgation of a new list, it would be mandatory for them to be dismissed as principals when the Board of Examiners approved a new list. With the help of the NAACP Legal Defense Fund, Mercado and Chance proceeded to bring suit "to challenge the allegedly discriminatory licensing tests and to seek an injunction against issuing of a new eligible list."[19]

The historical background of *Chance* goes back to 1898, when the New York State Legislature created the Board of Examiners to serve with independent authority as the examining unit of the New York City Board of Education. The Board of Examiners are accountable to the State Commissioner of Education and perform according to the state constitutional guidelines of "merit and fitness."[20]

When a vacancy for a supervisory position occurred in the New York City school system, it was required to be filled by the appointment of one of the three individuals on the top of the present list as a result of the examination. Moreover, until the list was exhausted or had expired at the end of four years no new examinations could be given.[21]

The Decentralization Law of 1970 resulted in a significant shift in these procedures. Under the new law, the community school boards could appoint supervisory personnel regardless of their ranking on the eligible list.[22]

Minorities and women were clearly not the individuals benefitting from the existing supervisory examination system. Rather, white candidates were overwhelmingly selected for principal positions. The results of these examinations highlighted the pattern of discrimination which existed in the selection process and the exclusionary aspects of the civil service system.

The plaintiffs in *Chance v. Board of Examiners*[23] challenged the selection procedures for principals and other supervisory personnel in the New York City school system on the ground that they were unconstitutionally discriminatory. Judge Walter R. Mansfield immediately issued a temporary restraining order preventing the board of examiners from issuing any new lists for supervisors. They were permitted, however, to continue administering the examinations. The plaintiffs then attempted "to obtain a preliminary injunction extending the temporary injunction up until the trial date (and, if possible, expanding the scope of the temporary order to prohibit further examinations)."[24]

In granting the preliminary injunction, the District Court found sufficient evidence in violation of the equal protection clause of the Fourteenth Amendment. Judge Mansfield held "that evidence did not establish that examinations, which had de facto effect of discriminating against black and Puerto Rican applicants . . . could be justified as necessary to obtain assistant principals and supervisors possessing required skills and qualifications."[25]

A survey by the court showed that of the 1,000 licensed principals in the New York City public schools, only eleven (or approximately 1 percent) were black, and only one was Puerto Rican. Moreover, of the 750 licensed principals in elementary schools, only five were black, and none at the time were Puerto Rican.[26]

The survey also revealed that whites passed the principal's examination almost one-and-a-half times as frequently as blacks and Puerto Ricans. Whites passed the test for assistant principal twice as frequently as blacks and Puerto Ricans. For assistant principal of day elementary schools, whites passed at one-third greater frequency than blacks and Puerto Ricans. The assistant principalships were important because they were the traditional route to the principal positions.[27]

While the District Court ruling effectively ceased the administration of the supervisory examination system, the examiners appealed to the U.S. Court of Appeals, Second Circuit, but the court affirmed the ruling of the District Court.[28] In July 1973, the plaintiffs obtained a final judgment against the defendants, permanently enjoining the operation of the old examination system, permitting all supervisory positions to be filled by acting personnel or by appointment of state licensed personnel, and allowing New York City Community School Boards or the Central Board of Education to select and appoint such supervisory personnel. Within six months of the effective date of the judgment, the defendants were to develop a plan for a permanent examination system.[29] The July 1973 decision was appealed by the examiners to the Court of Appeals, but was affirmed in April 1974.[30]

Judge Harold R. Tyler took over the case from Judge Mansfield in the midst of a controversy concerning the interim procedures. In March 1975, despite unresolved differences, the permanent plan was adopted, and for the first time the New York City school system would be required to include performance evaluation as a major component.[31]

In April 1975 Judge Milton Pollack took over the case from Judge Tyler and ordered a modified permanent plan. He believed that the administration of on-the-job performance tests should remain with the board of examiners, rather than be reassigned to the community school boards. Soon after Judge Pollack submitted his order, the U.S. Court of Appeals, Second Circuit, reviewed it and vacated it. The court ruled that both the permanent plan and the modified plan satisfied federal law requirements, and that the remaining issues regarding the establishment of a permanent examination system should be decided under state law. The Second Circuit instructed Judge Pollack to end jurisdiction by June 1978.[32]

In response to the Second Circuit's order to resolve the issues in the permanent plan by administrative and political procedures, the board of education passed a resolution in 1978 establishing "transitory" procedures, which did not include permanent licenses.

In October 1978, the Council of Supervisors and Administrators (CSA) brought suit in state court, in which they asked the court to permit the appointment of individuals who held licenses issued under the old examination to vacant positions on a permanent basis. These licenses had been declared invalid in previous court decisions. The state court decided to reinstate the interim procedures from the *Chance* 1973 Final Judgment.

The parties returned to Judge Pollack and requested that he review the 1973 Final Judgment in *Chance*. He did this and entered an order reinstating the interim procedures until December 31, 1980. This consent order also mandated that the chancellor arrange for new examinations in accordance with New York State and federal law and rules. He was to do this in cooperation with the board of examiners.[33]

The board of examiners proceeded with this mandate to develop examinations. They hired a consultant to prepare the junior high school principal examination, and two other principal examinations were developed by the staff at the board of examiners. In December 1980, the examiners announced the results of the licensing examination for assistant principal, junior high school. The results indicated that the failure rate for minorities was 90 percent, as compared to 50 percent for whites.[34]

On August 3, 1981, Frank J. Macchiarola, Chancellor of the New York City school system, filed suit in the United States District Court for the Southern District of New York,[35] alleging that the examinations for high school and junior high school principals, given in 1980, were racially discriminatory. The complaint attempted to prevent the board of examiners from appointing persons who passed the 1980 examinations for high school and junior high school principal, and from promulgating any future lists for licensing supervisory personnel until the examiners demonstrated that examinations, which were the basis of this selection procedure, were not racially discriminatory and were job-related.[36]

The basis for the suit was the results of the 1980 junior high school and high school principals' examination, which found that in the junior high school examination whites passed four times as frequently as blacks, almost three times as frequently as Hispanics, almost five times as frequently as Asians, and white men passed almost three times as frequently as white women. The results of the written portion of the high school examination illustrated the negative impact upon minorities applying for licenses as high school principals. Whites passed five times as frequently as blacks and more than three and a half times as frequently as Hispanics. On March 23, 1981, the final results of the high school examination were publicized and it appeared that 28 percent of the whites passed while no blacks or Hispanics passed.[37]

Macchiarola et al. v. Board of Examiners highlights some critical data concerning the period in which it was not required for supervisors to be chosen from the lists promulgated by the board of examiners. As cited earlier, in 1969 the New York City public schools were composed of approximately 1,000 licensed principals, only eleven (or approximately 1 percent) were black, and only one was Puerto Rican. During the eight years in which the interim system was in effect and the local community school boards were permitted to appoint principals under the decentralization law, minority representation in principal positions increased by 1979 to 5.6 percent Hispanics and 19.9 percent blacks. The interim system, however, terminated on December 30, 1981.[38]

On July 19, 1982, Judge Robert J. Ward handed down a consent order in the case of *Macchiarola et al. v. Board of Examiners*. The court ruled that the board of examiners should maintain responsibility for the development and administration of the junior high school and high school principal examinations, and the promulgation of lists. An adverse impact analysis, however, would be required to be undertaken by the examiners before such eligible lists were promulgated. No permanent supervisory appointments were to be made until the new lists were created, and in the interim, appointing authorities were permitted to make "conditional assignments." The court intended that the administration of examinations and the promulgation of the lists be completed as soon as possible.[39]

In an interview with the Legal Counsel of the New York City Board of Education on November 9, 1983 (almost sixteen months after Judge Ward's consent order), to determine the status of *Macchiarola et al. v. Board of Examiners*, the counsel indicated that the board of examiners had not as yet promulgated the lists for supervisory positions. The task of developing the examinations was given over to the consultants who had not devised the examinations. Everyone was being assigned to these supervisory positions on an acting basis. The legal counsel at the board of education was not optimistic regarding the resolution of this issue and believed that the solution might have to be a legislative one.[40]

The *Chance* decision had an important impact on the recruitment of minorities as principals in the New York City school system. Even though resistance to change was still evident, the fact that court action prompted the elimination of a barrier, in the form of an examination, made it easier for community school boards to appoint minority principals. In examining the hypothesis of this study that the rigid structure of municipal civil service systems and the principle of meritocracy underlying that system have contributed to and maintained a system of social inequity, it is relevant to observe that court action can effect change toward achieving social equity.

GUARDIANS ASSOCIATION OF NEW YORK V. CIVIL SERVICE COMMISSION

The settlement of *Guardians Association of New York v. Civil Service Commission*[41] involves four cases relating to different subject matter, but all concerning the selection of personnel in the New York City Police Department.

In the oldest of these *Guardians*[42] cases, the plaintiffs alleged that examination #8155 had a discriminatory effect on black and Hispanic candidates in their efforts to be appointed as entry-level police officers in the New York City Police Department. The court ruled that the defendants were in violation of Title VII of the Civil Rights Act of 1964, and ordered the defendants to achieve in the long term, 30 percent representation in the police force by blacks and Hispanics, and in the short term, 50 percent representation by these groups in entry-level police officer positions. Examination #8155 was to be used as the pool. On appeal, the Court of Appeals stated that "we affirm the District Court's finding that the City's specific use of the test violates Title VII, but vacate the remedy and remand for entry of a revised decree."[43]

During the period that the case was on appeal another examination (#1010) for entry-level positions was administered. Blacks and Hispanics comprised 35.4 percent of those taking the examination, and 28.5 percent of those passing. Using rank order as a basis for appointment would yield an 18 percent representation by blacks and Hispanics of the 8,000 top ranked candidates. Plaintiffs argued that examination #1010 violated Title VII, as did the prior examination; the city argued the opposite.[44]

While the parties were preparing for trial, negotiations for settlement were continuing, and on August 6, 1981, a settlement was signed and filed by the parties. The agreement called for the rank order eligibility list of those who passed examination #1010 with the accepted score of 64 to be divided into two parts. The plan indicated that:

All candidates scoring equal to or higher than the 12,000th person on the list are to be randomly selected by computer for further processing for selection for appointment to the January, 1982 class of the Police Academy. Candidates in this group not selected, unless rejected for failure to meet other requirements, are to receive priority consideration for appointment to entry level positions above all other candidates on the #1010 eligibility list. All the remaining candidates scoring 64 or above are to be randomly selected for appointment as the need arises.

It is anticipated that 3500 to 4500 appointments are to be made within the next two years and that the list will be exhausted.[45]

Under the settlement the city was required to develop a validity study to determine "the degree of correlation between how well a candidate performed on examination #1010 and how well the candidate, if appointed, subsequently performs as a police officer."[46]

Two of the other cases included in the settlement, *The Hispanic Society, et al. v. Civil Service Commission of the City of New York, et al.*,[47] and *Policewomen's Endowment Association, et al. v. Civil Service Commission of the City of New York, et al.*,[48] were filed on behalf of blacks, Hispanics, and women who either failed the promotional examination for sergeant (#8539) or passed with too low a score to realistically expect appointment. *The Hispanic Society* alleged that the test had a racially discriminatory impact on blacks and Hispanics and violated Title VII of the Civil Rights Act of 1964; *Policewomen* alleged gender-based discrimination under Title VII. Both cases sought injunctive relief to prevent the city from using the rank order results of the examination.[49]

The fourth case, *United States v. City of New York, et al.*,[50] alleged "that the city was engaged in a pattern or practice of discrimination against women, blacks and Hispanics in the selection and promotion of police officers in the New York City Police Department in violation of Title VII."[51] The government sought to enjoin this pattern and practice.

While the parties were preparing for trial a settlement was agreed upon on June 22, 1981, and all three of these cases were consolidated. The agreement permitted promotion to sergeant from eligibility list #8539 in accordance with the following modifications:

Of all the applicants taking examination #8539, 2.38 percent were women, 9.29 percent were black and 3.89 percent were Hispanics. The agreement provides that of the appointments made in each successive class or group of appointments from the eligibility list, 2.38 percent shall be women, 9.29 percent shall be black and 3.89 percent shall be Hispanic. The city agrees to promote all women, blacks, and Hispanics on eligibility list #8539 to achieve these percentages of female, black and Hispanic police sergeants. When the eligibility list of women, blacks and Hispanics is exhausted, the city agrees to seek additional women, blacks and Hispanic applicants for promotion by lowering by one score level the cut off point for placement on eligibility list #8539. The process is to be repeated when necessary until the appropriate number of qualified female, black and Hispanic candidates to meet the agreed upon percentages have been secured.[52]

It should be noted that the City of New York did not concede that there was any discrimination with regard to the selection of police sergeants.

The District Court decided that affirmative relief would be granted based upon the defendant's administration of examination #8155 and prior employment practices. These practices relate to the use of police tests administered between 1968 and 1970. The District Court observed,

The continued use of the results of those exams after 1972 when Title VII was amended to include municipal employers, had previously been found to violate Title VII because the exams had a disparate racial impact and were not job-related.[53]

The Court of Appeals ruled that "it would be contrary to Title VII's provision allowing the use of valid exams to hold that once an employer tries to construct such an exam and fails, any further failure to develop a valid exam constitutes intentional discrimination."[54] The court held that such intentional discrimination was absent, and since affirmative relief requires a pattern of prior discrimination, the court ordered that the affirmative hiring provisions be set aside and remanded to the District Court to devise new selection procedures.

The results of the examinations from 1968 to 1970, which the District Court used to demonstrate discriminatory effect, appear to be quite glaring. The results of the entry-level police officer examination #9080 showed that whites passed 1.59 times as frequently as blacks and 1.95 times as frequently as Hispanics. The results for promotional tests were more dramatic. Of those taking the sergeant's examination on April 12, 1969, whites passed 2.75 times as frequently as blacks and 6.6 times as frequently as Hispanics. The results of those taking the promotional

Table 7
Representation by Blacks in Large City Police Forces, 1972

A City	B Black Population %	C Black Police %	Equality Coefficient Column C/ Column B
Los Angeles	17.9	15.0	.84
Washington	70.0	37.0	.53
Chicago	33.0	16.2	.49
Miami	22.7	11.0	.48
Phoenix	5.0	2.0	.40
St. Louis	41.0	14.8	.36
Detroit	45.0	13.0	.29
New York	31.0	8.7	.28

SOURCE: The Guardians Association of New York City Police Department, Inc., The Hispanic Society of the New York City Police Department, Inc., et al., v. Civil Service Commission of the City of New York, et al., 72 Civ. 928 (S.D.N.Y. 1972), "Memorandum of Law in Support of Plaintiffs' Motion for a Preliminary Injunction," p. 30.

examination for lieutenant, given on February 28, 1970, showed that the passing rate for whites was 10.6 times that for blacks.[55]

At the time these examinations were administered considerable disparity existed between minority representation in the New York City Police Department and in the population at large. Table 7 illustrates how these data compare unfavorably with other large cities.

The results of the readministration of the examination for promotion to police sergeant (examination #2548) in June 1983 indicated that only 1.6 percent of the black and 4.4 percent of the Hispanic police officers who took the exam passed, as compared with 10.6 percent of the white police officers.[56] Despite the city's reluctance to a settlement with a quota, the mayor agreed to do so because of the city's lack of confidence in defending the test.[57]

The courts have had an impact in these police cases in highlighting the discriminatory effect of police examinations on minorities. Even with court action, however, the civil service system has been resistant to change. But without the intervention of the courts it is questionable whether the selection procedures for police officer positions would be restructured to enhance the opportunities for equity in the system.

BERKMAN V. CITY OF NEW YORK

In 1979, Brenda Berkman brought a class-action suit, on behalf of herself and other similarly situated women, against the City of New York and the New York City Fire Department. Berkman alleged that the examinations for entry-level firefighter position discriminated against women and sought declaratory and injunctive relief.

On March 4, 1982, District Court Judge Charles P. Sifton ruled that the examinations discriminated against women and did not meet the job-related validity tests needed to perform well as a firefighter. The action was brought pursuant to Title VII of the Civil Rights Act of 1964 and the Fourteenth Amendment to the Constitution.[58] The order was affirmed on appeal by the United States Court of Appeals on March 29, 1983.[59]

Berkman and the class of women she represented had failed the physical portion of the entry-level firefighters examination #3040. In ruling for the plaintiff Judge Sifton held that the:

(1) physical portion of the exam had a disparate impact on women and was not sufficiently job related to rebut prima facie case of sex discrimination; (2) female applicant and class were entitled to injunction prohibiting appointments based on exam results as well as interim relief in form of an order directing the sending of notice of appointments to up to 45 unsuccessful female applicants; and (3) evidence did not support finding that discrimination in connection with the examination was intentional or that there had been a demonstrated pattern of significant prior discrimination so as to require the various defendants, if there were not a sufficient number of unsuccessful female applicants under the exam still interested in position of fire fighter to fill the number of positions that would have been filled by women under sex-neutral examination, to affirmatively recruit and appoint women for those positions.[60]

Insofar as the court concluded that the physical portion of Examination #3040 was sexually discriminatory and ordered the preparation of a new physical test which does not discriminate against women, it may be worthy of note to examine the background of Examination #3040.

On January 12, 1973, groups representing black and Hispanic firefighters brought suit in the United States District Court for the Southern District of New York, alleging that Examination #0159 (entry-level firefighter position) had an adverse impact on blacks and Hispanics.[61] They sought to prevent New York City from appointing firefighters from List #0159. Judge Edward Weinfeld held that Examination #0159 was unconstitutional under the Fourteenth Amendment because of its discriminatory impact on blacks and Hispanics and ruled that the city could not make further appointments based on the results of the test. Subsequently, Judge Weinfeld directed defendants "to proceed expeditiously to prepare a new examination for the position of fireman which did not discriminate against blacks and Hispanics in accordance with professionally accepted methods of test preparation."[62]

It was this examination, prepared in response to the *Vulcan Society* class action, which Brenda Berkman took, examination #3040. The results of the test were as follows:

The written test was given on December 3, 1977, to 25,168 persons: 24,758 males and 410 females. (It is these 410 women who constitute the class, as presently defined.) A total of 24,252 males and 389 females passed the written test. The physical exam was administered over the period February 15, 1978 to April 30, 1978 to a total of 18,148 persons: 18,060 males and 88 females. Of these, 16,925 males and 79 females completed the physical test. A total of 7,847 males and no females passed the test.[63]

These figures indicate that 26 percent of the men who passed the written exam did not appear for the physical exam, while close to 77 percent of the women who passed the written test did not appear to take the physical exam. It appears that publicity campaigns indicating that the physical test was too difficult for women to pass were effective in deterring many of those women who successfully passed the written test from trying. Of those candidates, however, who did take the physical examination, 46 percent of the men passed while none of the women did.[64]

In evaluating the impact of the civil service examinations on women candidates for the position of firefighter the court held that in *Berkman* as in *Guardians*, "The exam at issue had a disparate impact by any reasonable measure including the standards developed by the Supreme Court . . . and by the Equal Employment Opportunity Commission ("EEOC") in its Uniform Guidelines on Employee Selection Procedures."[65] Thus, the court enjoined the defendants from use of the eligibility list promulgated from Examination #3040, and ordered that "notices of appointment shall be sent to up to 45 of those women who in 1977 and 1978 applied to become firefighters and who are found to be qualified for appointment and willing to be appointed."[66] The determination of qualification was to be based upon the new physical test which the court ordered to be prepared.

It is worthy of note that of approximately 70 women who took the new physical examination, 40 women were appointed probationary firefighters in September 1982. Brenda Berkman was included in this group. A follow-up on the status of the women who were appointed to the fire department indicates that Brenda Berkman and Zaida Gonzalez were dismissed as firefighters by the New York City Fire Department. The case returned to Judge Charles P. Sifton in Federal District Court in Brooklyn. In reinstating Berkman and Gonzalez, as probationary firefighters, with back pay, Judge Sifton stated that the court found "extraordinary evidence of intentional discrimination."[67]

The District Court ordered the city to devise a new physical examination which would be administered as part of the next exam (#1162). But the city was unable to reach agreement on a new exam and proceeded in 1983 to administer a test based on the 1982 exam. In 1985 Judge Sifton ruled[68] that the scoring system used in this exam placed undue emphasis on speed and discriminated against women applicants. He ordered the city to develop a new scoring system combining the written and physical portion of the exam which would have greater validity than the current exam and have the least adverse affect against women applicants.

On February 17, 1987, however, the United States Court of Appeals made a decision[69] which weakened the 1982 ruling in *Berkman*. The Court of Appeals ruled that the new test (which Judge Sifton ruled discriminated against women) was valid, in that immediate speed and strength are legitimate measures to test for in potential firefighters, and that the process used by the city to develop the exam was legal. [70] The plaintiffs appealed to the United States Supreme Court because of the diminished opportunity for women to be hired as firefighters if this decision stands, but the Court refused to hear the case.[71]

Despite the recent setback, the lower courts achieved a degree of success, in *Berkman*, in challenging the municipal civil service system in that they were able to force the fire department to change the physical portion of the firefighters' examination in order to expand the opportunity for recruiting more women as firefighters. By finding these examinations to have a discriminatory effect on women, the courts exposed the exclusionary aspects of the selection process in civil service and made possible the hiring of women as firefighters.

CONCLUSIONS

The purpose of this chapter was to review several court cases that challenged civil service examination procedures and selection devices on the ground that they are unconstitutional insofar as they discriminate against minorities and women. Other mechanisms for instituting change had not proven effective, and so the courts were seen as a potential instrument for mandating the elimination of structural barriers to achieving social equity in municipal civil service systems. The major thrust in the selected cases reviewed here demonstrates that these courts found the selection procedures in the civil service systems to be inequitable. In dealing with these inequities they have attempted to structure remedial action.

The courts have played a significant role with regard to equal access to public employment. They have been the prime agents in efforts to bring social equity to municipal civil service systems. Personnel administrators have been associated to a greater degree with maintaining the status quo in terms of the use of merit principles to protect the incumbent civil servants than to adjust entrance requirements which might serve to increase representation by minorities and women in civil service jobs. Perhaps the role of the courts in attempting to achieve social equity will serve as an example and motivation for public administrators to see the compatibility of merit and equity principles.[72]

NOTES

1. Marilyn Gittell, "Putting Merit Back in the Merit System," *Social Policy* 3 (September/October 1972): 21.

2. *Griggs v. Duke Power Co.*, 401 U.S. 424 (1971).

3. Michael A. Rebell and Arthur R. Block, *Educational Policy Making and the Courts: An Empirical Study of Judicial Activism* (Chicago: University of Chicago Press, 1982), p. 14.

4. E. Richard Larson, "Discriminatory Selection Devices in Public Employment Systems," *Good Government*, Winter 1971, p. 6.

5. Ibid.

6. Elizabeth Bartholet, "Application of Title VII to Jobs in High Places," *Harvard Law Review* 95 (March 1982): 949.

7. Project for Academic Affirmative Action Training, "Principles of Employment Discrimination Law—Constitutional Protections, Statutes, Administrative Orders and Rules and Court Decisions Which May Be Relevant to Employment Practices or Higher Education Facilities," Washington, D.C., n.d., pp. 9–10. (Mimeographed.)

8. Ibid., pp. 16–21.

9. Gittell, "Putting Merit Back in the Merit System," p. 21.

10. *Griggs v. Duke Power Co.*, 292 F. Supp. 243 (M.D.N.C. 1968).

11. *Griggs v. Duke Power Co.*, 402 F. 2d (4th Cir. 1970); for more extensive background on the case see Herbert N. Bernhardt, "Griggs v. Duke Power Co.: The Implications for Private and Public Employers," *Texas Law Review* 50 (May 1972): 901–929.

12. *Griggs*, 401 U.S. 424.

13. Larson, "Discriminatory Selection Devices in Public Employment Systems," p. 3.

14. Ibid.

15. Bartholet, "Application of Title VII to Jobs in High Places," p. 957.

16. Ibid., p. 959.

17. *Chance v. Board of Exam. and the Board of Ed. of City of New York,* 330 F. Supp. 203 (S.D.N.Y. 1971); it should be noted that litigation related to this case has spanned more than ten years.

18. Legal Action Center of the City of New York, "Report on Activities," March 1975, p. 5. (Mimeographed.)

19. Rebell and Block, *Educational Policy Making and the Courts,* pp. 76–77.

20. N.Y. Constitution, Art. V, §6 (1953), quoted in "Discriminatory Merit Systems: A Case Study of the Supervisory Examinations Administered by the New York Board of Examiners," *Columbia Journal of Law and Social Problems* 6 (September 1970): 375.

21. Rebell and Block, *Educational Policy Making and the Courts,* p. 76.

22. Ibid.

23. *Chance v. Board of Examiners,* 330 F. Supp. 203.

24. Rebell and Block, *Educational Policy Making and the Courts,* p. 81.

25. *Chance v. Board of Examiners,* 330 F. Supp. at 204.

26. *Chance v. Board of Examiners,* 330 F. Supp. at 208.

27. *Chance v. Board of Examiners,* 330 F. Supp. at 210.

28. *Chance v. Board of Examiners,* 458 F. 2d 1167 (2nd Cir. 1972).

29. *Chance v. Board of Examiners,* 70 Civ. 4141 (S.D.N.Y. 1973).

30. *Chance v. Board of Education of City of New York,* 496 F. 2d 820 (2nd Cir. 1974).

31. Rebell and Block, *Educational Policy Making and the Courts,* p. 83.

32. Ibid., pp. 84–85; and *Chance v. Board of Examiners,* 561 F. 2d 1079 (2nd Cir. 1977).

33. Rebell and Block, *Educational Policy Making and the Courts,* pp. 120–121.

34. Ibid.

35. *Macchiarola et al. v. Board of Examiners,* 81 Civ. 4798 (S.D.N.Y. August 3, 1981), "Complaint."

36. Rebell and Block, *Educational Policy Making and the Courts,* p. 122.

37. *Macchiarola et al. v. Board of Examiners,* 81 Civ. 4798 (S.D.N.Y. August 5, 1981), "Memorandum in Support of Plaintiffs' Motion for a Temporary Restraining Order, a Preliminary Injunction and an Order for Accelerated Discovery," pp. 9, 12, 16.

38. Ibid., p. 16.

39. *Macchiarola et al. v. Board of Examiners,* 81 Civ. 4798 (S.D.N.Y. July 19, 1982), "Order," p. 7.

40. Telephone interview with Carol Ziegler, Legal Counsel, Board of Education, New York City, 9 November 1983.

41. *Guardians Ass'n of N.Y. v. Civil Ser. Com'n,* 527 F. Supp. 751 (S.D.N.Y. 1981).

42. *The Guardians Association of the New York City Police Department, Inc., the Hispanic Society of the New York City Police Department, Inc., et al. v. Civil Service Commission of the City of New York, et al.*, 72 Civ. 928 (S.D.N.Y. 1972).

43. *Guardians Ass'n of New York City v. Civil Serv.*, 630 F. 2d 79 (2nd Cir. 1980).

44. *Guardians v. Civil Service Commission*, 527 F. Supp. at 753.

45. *Guardians v. Civil Service Commission*, 527 F. Supp. at 753.

46. *Guardians v. Civil Service Commission*, 527 F. Supp. at 753.

47. *The Hispanic Society, et al. v. Civil Service Commission of the City of New York, et al.*, 80 Civ. 5603 (S.D.N.Y. 1980).

48. *Policewomen's Endowment Association, et al. v. Civil Service Commission of the City of New York, et al.*, 81 Civ. 0537 (S.D.N.Y. 1981).

49. *Guardians v. Civil Service Commission*, 527 F. Supp. at 754.

50. *United States v. City of New York, et al.*, 81 Civ. 4510 (S.D.N.Y. 1981).

51. *Guardians v. Civil Service Commission*, 527 F. Supp. at 754.

52. *Guardians v. Civil Service Commission*, 527 F. Supp. at 755.

53. *Guardians v. Civil Service*, 630 F. 2d at 111.

54. *Guardians v. Civil Service*, 630 F. 2d at 112.

55. *The Guardians Association of the New York City Police Department, Inc., the Hispanic Society of the New York City Police Department, Inc., et al., v. Civil Service Commission of the City of New York, et al.*, 72 Civ. 928 (S.D.N.Y. 1972), "Memorandum of Law in Support of Plaintiffs' Motion for a Preliminary Injunction," p. 14.

56. Joyce Purnick, "City to Use Racial Quota to Pick at Least 1,000 Police Sergeants," *New York Times*, 11 November 1985, sec. A, p. 1.

57. "Koch: Fighting Suit Posed Major Risks," *The Chief-Leader*, 25 April 1986, p. 10. The U.S. Supreme Court has agreed to review an appeal by white police officers seeking promotion to sergeant who claim that they have been discriminated against as a result of the settlement.

58. *Berkman v. City of New York*, 536 F. Supp. 177 (E.D.N.Y. 1982).

59. *Berkman v. City of New York*, 705 F. 2d 584 (2nd Cir. 1983).

60. *Berkman v. City of New York*, 536 F. Supp. at 178.

61. *Vulcan Society v. Civil Service Commission*, 360 F. Supp. 1265 (S.D.N.Y. 1973), affirmed in part and remanded 490 F. 2d 387 (2nd Cir. 1973).

62. *Berkman v. City of New York*, 536 F. Supp. at 183.

63. *Berkman v. City of New York*, 536 F. Supp. at 200.

64. *Berkman v. City of New York*, 536 F. Supp. at 204.

65. *Berkman v. City of New York*, 536 F. Supp. at 205.

66. *Berkman v. City of New York*, 536 F. Supp. at 218.

67. Philip Shenon, "2 Women Win Bias Suit Against Fire Dept.," *New York Times*, 9 December 1983, sec. A, p. 1.

68. *Berkman v. City of New York*, 626 F. Supp. 591 (E.D.N.Y. 1985).

69. *Berkman v. City of New York*, 812 F. 2d 52 (2nd Cir. 1987).

70. "Ruling Could Curtail Hiring New Women in Fire Department," *New York Times*, 14 April 1987, sec. A, p. 1.

71. "Court Refuses Suit by Women Over Fire Test," *New York Times*, 6 October 1987, sec. A, p. 1. The decision of the Supreme Court to refuse hearing arguments on this case does not have national implication beyond the New York City case in that the justices did not give their reasons for refusing to hear the appeal.

72. Eugene B. McGregor, Jr., "Social Equity and the Public Service," *Public Administration Review* 34 (January/February 1974): 28.

Challenges to the Merit System: Public Employment Programs

5

Since the Great Depression of the 1930s, the government has used public service employment programs as a device for hiring the chronically unemployed. These programs attempted to present structural alternatives to the normal civil service procedure in order to accomplish certain employment goals. Public employment programs would appear to solve the unemployment problems of minorities and the structurally unemployed, but the few efforts in this area challenge the notion that government employment is the solution to unemployment problems. In examining the potential for public employment programs to be effective in hiring minorities and the structurally unemployed in permanent jobs in cities, it is necessary to recognize the inflexibility of municipal civil service systems and begin to devise legislation that eliminates barriers in civil service in order to facilitate the recruitment of the structurally unemployed.[1]

The Great Depression was a traumatic event in American history. Unemployment rolls had reached unprecedented numbers. In 1929, 3 percent of the workforce was unemployed; by

1933, unemployment reached 25 percent. From 1931 to 1940, unemployment never fell below 14 percent, and for four of those years it averaged more than 20 percent.[2]

Accounts of economic distress, discontent, and desperation were prevalent throughout the country. The direction that this dissatisfaction would take was to depend on the inclination of government to act in response to the disorder.[3] Whether or not government employment could be used to solve unemployment problems would be an issue for the future.

The New Deal

The moving force in an attempt to restore stability was Franklin Delano Roosevelt, who conceptualized the New Deal and organized the coalition to back it in his attempt to win the Democratic nomination and the 1932 election.[4]

To counter the Depression, the Roosevelt administration created a series of work-relief programs from 1930 to 1940. It was the Federal Emergency Relief Act (FERA), signed May 12, 1933, that provided relief for many unemployed. The federal government broke all precedents in relief-giving; it assumed responsibility for relief and distributed large sums of money for this purpose. During the three years in which the program existed (May 1933 to June 1936), the federal government allocated $3 billion for direct relief.[5] By January 1935, however, the political climate was pressing for substitution of work relief for direct relief. As early as October 1934 Roosevelt publicly announced that direct relief should be abolished.[6]

In January 1935, President Roosevelt asked Congress for $4.8 billion for direct work relief. The unemployed would build roads, sidewalks, parks, playgrounds, water mains, and other public works. Roosevelt's request to Congress for so much money for a single purpose was unprecedented by any previous president. Congress, however, approved the funding within four months, and "the Works Progress Administration—the most controversial of the New Deal programs—was under way."[7] Roosevelt appointed Harry Hopkins administrator of the Works Progress Administration (WPA).[8]

In discussing the controversy concerning federal job creation programs in more recent times, many still believe that the federal government should transfer funds to state and local governments for the purpose of eliminating unemployment and simultaneously expanding services to the constituencies. Moreover, proponents of public service employment argue that jobs, not merely monetary relief, are essential to the self-respect of individuals.[9]

It is worth noting that while the New Deal jobs were able to bypass civil service requirements the structure functioned primarily outside of the civil service. Most of these jobs were conceived of as being temporary.

The WPA

The Works Progress Administration (WPA) is often used as a model for proposing the creation of newly created public sector jobs for unemployed persons. What is significant about the WPA is that unlike its predecessor, the Federal Employment Relief Administration (FERA), it paid an hourly wage for work performed, even if the total was greater than a welfare payment. While WPA programs included minority and female representation, the programs were not designed with that as a goal. In addition, employment opportunities in the WPA ranged from unskilled to highly skilled occupations.[10]

President Roosevelt wanted to include the WPA in the civil service and to that end issued Executive Order 7916 extending the civil service requirements to all government agencies which were previously excluded. But a joint Congressional resolution of February 4, 1939, extending WPA appropriations forbade this. WPA employees were considered emergency employees, thereby exempt from civil service requirements. Thus, WPA administrators and workers operated outside the civil service. The fitness of workers was determined by those who appointed them. Exams were oral or written. The written exam was to be a practical one to demonstrate knowledge of the job. A practical demonstration of a trade as required was usually oral as there were no shops with which to demonstrate skills.[11]

Classification of jobs was similar to the civil service, and salaries were on par with the Classification Act of 1923.[12] It appears, however, that the civil service rolls were never opened to WPA workers, which suggests that permanent civil service status for the workers was not a goal of the program. Workers were expected to return to private industry as soon as openings occurred.

The status of women in these programs is somewhat ambiguous, as heads of families were given preference over women. In 1936, however, women were represented nationally by 52.8 percent of the total employed on clerical projects, 56.7 percent on professional and technical projects, and 63.2 percent on educational projects.[13]

Data on racial or religious characteristics were largely omitted from WPA application forms in an effort to prevent discrimination. In his Executive Order 7046, of May 20, 1935, President Roosevelt stressed that assignment to work would be free of discrimination.[14] Statistics available from February 1939 indicate that 14 percent of the total number of workers certified for WPA employment were blacks. This figure varied greatly from state to state.[15]

Evaluation of the WPA suggests that while the number of people hired were significant, this remedy did not begin to meet the scope of the problem. During the first five years of operation WPA provided an average of approximately 2 million jobs. But even at its peak, only about one in four unemployed had WPA jobs.[16]

Full Employment Legislation

World War II, however, obviated the need for the creation of additional public service jobs. The period during World War II experienced the longest era of full employment ever known in this country. Clearly, a shortage of workers helped the ranks of unemployed. Full employment also served to help individuals leave the poverty ranks.[17]

Full employment, however, did not fade the memory of the Depression. And the Full Employment Bill of 1945 was introduced in Congress by liberal senators in response to their concern for jobs. Congress defeated the bill despite Senate approval by 75 to 0. Conservatives in the House of Representatives were evidently unwilling to accept the notion of the "right of employment." What emerged was the Employment Act of 1946. This weaker bill, however, called for the federal government to create employment opportunities for those willing and able to work.[18]

An analysis of the legislation suggests that the defeat of the Full Employment Bill was clearly a mandate against the notion of government intervention with economic or job creation solutions to guarantee full employment. It reflected defeat for the idea that strong government was what was needed to eliminate unemployment. The Employment Act vaguely acknowledged the obligation by government for full employment, but it did not provide any mechanisms for providing a specific level of employment.[19]

Although unemployment levels since the passage of the Employment Act of 1946 have remained far below those of the Great Depression, they have been consistently higher than the unemployment levels of World War II.[20]

The Great Society Programs

What emerged in the 1960s, as a reaction to the "war on poverty," were Lyndon Johnson's Great Society programs. In order to effectively deal with problems in the inner city, the federal government chose to bypass state and local agencies and establish neighborhood structures to implement the funded programs. (This chapter will examine one of these programs, New Careers, which was an outgrowth of the Economic Opportunity Act of 1964 and the Elementary and Secondary Education Act of 1965.)

The basic structure of urban politics changed to encompass the creation of antipoverty councils and manpower agencies. As a result of federal guidelines mandating participation by the poor, blacks assumed responsibility and obtained jobs in many of these agencies, just as other immigrant groups controlled city departments. These federal programs effected the return of traditional processes of urban politics.[21]

What is important to focus on is not only the control blacks obtained over some of the new agencies, but the nature of the intervention by the federal government in city agencies. The federal government used these programs to prod city government into responding to blacks. The response was not always positive on the local level. While white politicians may have been upset about the notion of losing control of a great deal of patronage, they became exacerbated when the federal government allowed the new agencies to demand more services from city departments for blacks. In effect the Great Society programs changed the basic pattern of relationships among existing constituent groups in the city.[22]

These programs of the 1960s were particularly important because it was the first time that there was an effort to use employment programs to hire minorities. The new agencies attempted to bypass civil service restrictions.

The remainder of this chapter will focus on three special employment programs that attempted to present structural alternatives to the normal civil service procedure in order to accomplish certain employment goals; these programs include the Paraprofessional Programs (also known as New Careers), the Emergency Employment Act of 1971 (EEA), and the Comprehensive Employment and Training Act of 1973 (CETA). The origins, goals, performance, problems, and potential of these programs will be analyzed to illustrate which structures should be avoided and which encouraged in fulfilling the employment needs of the disadvantaged populations in cities.

PARAPROFESSIONALS

Given that the private sector has been unable to provide sufficient jobs for full employment in society, we must rely on the public sector for this function. It has been suggested that the paraprofessional model has had a significant impact on the notion that those who were once excluded from contributing to the community can work in important jobs. Data indicate that 500,000 to a million people are in paraprofessional jobs, which has had an influence on improved delivery of services in certain functional areas.[23] The paraprofessional concept (also known as new careers) as represented in the Public Service Careers Program encompasses the basic WPA idea of job creation, but adds a significant education and training component, as well as a direct career ladder.

Professionalism reduced opportunities for blacks and other minorities because of increased requirements and credentials. Paraprofessional programs dealt with that restriction. Initially, they served as a model for eliminating artificial barriers, in the form of credentials and requirements, which often exclude minorities and women from civil service jobs. The purpose of this section is to examine some of these paraprofessional programs, particularly in the fields of education and health, in order to analyze the paraprofessional concept as a public service employment scheme. The emphasis of this study will be on the employment and career aspects of the paraprofessional movement rather than with the impact of the paraprofessionals on improving human services.[24]

The passage of the Economic Opportunity Act in 1964 created the impetus for new career programs. In fulfilling the legislative mandate to insure "maximum feasible participation" of the poor in all parts of the Office of Economic Opportunity (OEO) program, including staffing, local community action agencies (CAAs) translated into many programs the concept of the aide. The CAAs were able to circumvent traditional public service recruitment patterns and requirements. Entrance requirements were eased, jobs were redesigned to fit the job to the worker, on-the-job training programs were instituted, and indigenous, noncredentialled, low-income adults were employed to work in fields traditionally professional in orientation.

The enactment of the Scheuer Amendment in 1965[25] and the increased attention given the new careers concept,[26] gave the paraprofessional movement programmatic impetus. Congress appropriated close to $35 million for the start of demonstration projects creating publicly financed jobs for the hard-core unemployed in such public service professions as health, education, welfare, and public safety. Linked to the new paraprofessional positions was the concept that training and education would be built in from the start to allow for career ladder advancement.[27]

Teacher Paraprofessionals

Since the start of the Elementary and Secondary Education Act (ESEA) Title I–funded teacher paraprofessional program, the recruitment and selection process has shifted from an open community-based system to a closed school-based system.

From 1967 to 1969, the Council Against Poverty and its delegate agencies (CAPs) were intimately involved in the recruitment and selection of teacher paraprofessionals. The intent of the process was to integrate community residents with backgrounds compatible with those of children in the neighborhood as personnel in the local schools.[28] The criteria used for selection of teacher paraprofessionals during this period were as follows:

1. Applicant's income shall meet poverty level index.
2. Applicant shall reside in local school zone.
3. Applicant shall be actively involved in community work.
4. Applicant shall demonstrate ability and willingness to work with children.[29]

A high school diploma was not required.

Two events contributed to the change in teacher paraprofessional recruitment and selection policies in New York City: (1) increased ESEA Title I funds, and (2) unionization of the teacher paraprofessionals. As funds from Title I increased, the role of the CAP agencies and the community disappeared, enabling the teacher paraprofessional program to become solely a board of education program. In addition, as the United Federation of Teachers (UFT) was selected as the bargaining unit, the role of the CAPs as representatives in the Board of Education bureaucracy was no longer necessary, because the UFT became solely responsible for negotiating for teacher paraprofessionals.

According to those interviewed, recruitment became a closed system, administered by the schools and checked by the union. The focus shifted from hiring low-income indigenous persons to hiring persons who demonstrated a desire to become teachers and who, in general, met the subjective criteria of the school principal. A high school diploma or equivalency became an informal requirement even though it was not formally specified in the board of education personnel manual. Criteria regarding neighborhood residency, poverty income, and community participation were virtually eliminated.

Despite the professional takeover of the recruitment and selection process which effectively limited the low-income unemployed person's access into the school hierarchy, the majority of the paraprofessionals entering the system continue to be either black or Puerto Rican. Historically, blacks and Puerto Ricans have been virtually excluded from the ranks of the school occupational structure. They are now very much a part of the school system as a result of the early teacher paraprofessional movement.[30] Their ranks, however, are at the lowest level of the system.

The concept of career advancement has been very much a part of the teacher paraprofessional movement in education. It appears, however, that promotion and salary increases are dependent upon (1) obtaining a credential and (2) accumulating college credit. A teacher paraprofessional who does not obtain a high school diploma or equivalent remains in the entry-level position of teacher aide, regardless of number of years of experience, on-the-job performance, or number in-service training programs attended. This approach effectively bars all noncredentialled and nonprofessionally oriented paraprofessionals from mobility in the school hierarchy. In addition, regardless of the number of in-service training sessions attended or the number of college credits obtained, a teacher paraprofessional remains in the entry-level, noncompetitive civil service slot until that person obtains a degree and becomes a licensed teacher.[31]

Despite apparent restrictiveness, the career ladder training programs are effective career mechanisms enabling paraprofessionals to become teachers. Alternative career advancement schemes ought to be instituted to enable all workers to move up the school hierarchy without formal educational requirements inhibiting the process.

Health Paraprofessionals

The health care programs in New York City reviewed in this study were all generated in the late 1960s under OEO grants, and although each program was separate and autonomous, policies regarding recruitment and selection were similar. Essentially, the criteria used for selection of paraprofessionals were (1) Community residency, (2) Poverty income level, and (3) Community consciousness. A high school diploma or equivalent was not required, except for the Health Extern job category.[32]

The recruitment and selection structure established by each program could be characterized as an open, agency-based system, which was checked by the community through the personnel committees of each of the agency's community boards of directors. Information regarding the employment needs of the agency was disseminated throughout the community via other agencies, neighborhood meetings, and advertisements in newspapers with a large minority readership. Final selection of candidates in two of the sample programs was carried out by members of the community board's personnel committee. In one program, selection was the responsibility of revolving teams composed of lay and professional staff.

Recruitment in the 1970s, however, shifted from an open system to a closed system. Recruitment of new paraprofessionals changed to a grapevine system (word-of-mouth advertising). Although this system was linked to the community, community-wide dissemination of job openings virtually stopped, restricting access to jobs to specific segments of the population.

Selection criteria in two sample programs seemed to shift upward in the latter part of 1970, when the more traditional Department of Health, Education, and Welfare (HEW) bureaucracy replaced OEO as the primary funding agent. Under OEO, for example, criteria used for selecting the directors of family planning clinics were similar to criteria used for selecting all family planning paraprofessionals. Under HEW guidelines, the directors were required to have a high school diploma or equivalent, plus two to three years experience supervising people, or an associate of arts degree. Similarly, all eighteen family planning clinics in New York City were urged, but not required, to give preference to applicants with high school diplomas when filling entry-level paraprofessional positions. The tendency to upgrade entrance requirements over time regardless of job function becomes evident.

Attempts to create a career ladder scheme have been limited, restricting upward movement to specific job categories created for paraprofessionals. Most of the programs employing health paraprofessionals were discrete programs with few job slots to start with, so that career advancement was limited by the size of the programs. In addition, occupational structure of most programs is such that for a health paraprofessional to obtain greater access to job mobility with the agency hierarchy necessitates the attainment of a credential and/or license or regular civil service status.

When the paraprofessional is faced with credential and licensing requirements, job mobility is virtually impossible regardless of experience. The Health Extern, for example, who performs a physician's function could not find a comparable position in any other health care institution. The Health Extern can only enter the private or public health hierarchy as a nurse's aide. The job title of Health Extern does not appear on the regular civil service listing, and there are no comparable titles on job descriptions which forsake civil service requirements or credentialling requirements. Despite the year's training Health Externs received in the practice of obstetrics and nursing, they were required to attend regular nursing school in order to obtain the position of Licensed Practical Nurse or Registered Nurse.

In addition, the rigid and conservative position taken by professional organizations and licensing agencies impose greater limitations on the mobility of the health paraprofessional. The push to professionalize presents a major barrier preventing health paraprofessionals' entrance into the major health occupations and institutions.

Conclusions

Increasingly, new services have been offered as a result of the utilization of paraprofessional workers.[33] However, training and career development opportunities are not keeping pace with the expanded roles and responsibilities of paraprofessionals.[34]

Despite some of the conditions outlined in this section, the paraprofessional concept as envisioned by new career advocates[35] could offer an appropriate model for public service employment if many of the obstacles highlighted could be overcome. All of the efforts, however, to bypass civil service requirements and professional credentials were ultimately coopted by the system using its own standards. Early on in the paraprofessional movement, professional associations and personnel people resisted the entrance of paraprofessionals into city agencies. The union, for example, opposed the paraprofessionals at first. However, they later saw the opportunity to recruit paraprofessionals as union members. Increased professionalization of teacher paraprofessionals can be observed as a result of integration with the union.

State and local governments have the responsibility to determine local public service needs and to develop strategies and priorities for meeting those needs. Municipalities have the opportunity to examine and restructure public service bureaucracies for the purpose of constructing a new occupational structure that adheres to the paraprofessional model by generating jobs that increase the quantity and quality of public services and broaden career possibilities for the unemployed poor.

THE EMERGENCY EMPLOYMENT ACT OF 1971

The Emergency Employment Act of 1971[36] (EEA) was the first major piece of federal legislation since the 1930s dealing with public employment. Public employment programs are relevant because among other attributes they can provide greater employment opportunity for minority and female unemployed than the private sector. The intent of the act, during 1972 and 1973, was to provide state and local governments with an estimated $2.25 billion to establish 150,000 transitional jobs for unemployed and underemployed workers.[37] EEA guidelines called for program agents to make "assurances that the program will, to the maximum extent feasible, contribute to the elimination of artificial barriers to employment and occupational advancement, including civil service requirements which restrict employment opportunities for the disadvantaged."[38] These requirements were to follow guidelines issued by the U.S. Civil Service Commission.

It is the aspect of the legislation relating to civil service requirements that is of particular interest. Since the hypothesis of this study suggests that the rigid structure of municipal civil service systems and the principle of meritocracy underlying that system have contributed to and maintained a system of social inequity, this section will, among other things, examine the impact of the Emergency Employment Act of 1971 as a challenge to the merit system and evaluate whether the programs were successful in eliminating any of the artificial barriers to employment opportunities for minority populations.

The role played by state and local governments can determine the success of the intended goals of the program. The program was intended to balance city government needs with increased employment in public service jobs by the hard-core unemployed. The city goals were directly linked to revenue sharing. The two goals, however, were not always compatible. Distribution of resources within a city is often tied to political priorities. Those unemployed groups with the greatest need are likely the least qualified for employment in the priority areas.[39]

Congress decided what individuals and groups would be hired under EEA. The intent of the original bills provided that the program be directed to the unemployed and the underemployed. While the legislation did not set priorities, it was geared toward broad interests. The general statement included groups which were identified as needing assistance through public service jobs. Those identified were low-income individuals, youth, recent veterans, and individuals in such industries as defense, aerospace, and construction, which were affected by shifts in federal spending.[40]

Case study material with regard to EEA in this section will emphasize the experience of several large cities.[41] The purpose of this comparison is to show the differences in implementation and results in EEA programs among the selected cities.

Planning and Implementation

According to Department of Labor guidelines, each city could organize the public employment program as it chose. One study observed, "Forty-five percent of the cities assigned this program to the personnel department, 21 percent to the manpower-planning unit, 17 percent to the office of mayor or city manager, and the other 17 percent to departments of human resources, planning, budget, or finance."[42]

It would seem that the distribution of jobs and policy making under EEA would be a matter of important city policy and would prompt decision making on a high level. This tone could be reflected in New York City in the initial planning period. The budget director was particularly influential in setting New York City priorities and translating those priorities into the distribution of jobs to agencies.[43]

Responsibility for implementation of the program was delegated to the Human Resources Administration, the Bureau of the Budget, and the Department of Personnel. While each agency had a particular responsibility, the Human Resources Administration as prime sponsor had responsibility for program operation.[44]

The decision to establish the administration of EEA in New York City in the Human Resources Administration (HRA) as opposed to the mayor's office had a considerable impact on the nature of the program. The rationale for the decision was based on the fact that HRA ran other employment operations. If EEA had been set up in the mayor's office it might have received greater status and flexibility and increased consideration of program goals. HRA viewed the program as a mechanism for making up budget cuts. Interviews with HRA staff indicated their unfamiliarity with the goals of EEA.[45]

Locating EEA within an existing agency also made it unfeasible for staff to promote changes in civil service policy. Response by the personnel department would be more realistic if the pressure came from the mayor's office. In cities where EEA was set up as a separate unit, the program was seen as being more important in terms of its ability to deal with the hard-core unemployed, and there was openness to the notion of changing civil service procedures to permit EEA participants to be placed in permanent civil service jobs in the future.[46]

In Chicago, the Mayor's Office for Manpower and the Personnel Department in the Civil Service Commission were responsible for implementation of the EEA program. However, when departmental requests for jobs exceeded Chicago's allocation, Mayor Daley appointed a committee to determine priorities. The members of the committee included the mayor's top administrative assistant, his assistant for manpower, the director of personnel, the budget officer, and the comptroller.[47]

In Milwaukee, Mayor Henry Maier assigned the Intergovernmental Fiscal Liaison Department the task of obtaining funds. But for the administration of the program he assigned the Civil Service Commission, which was already responsible for Public Service Careers and several other manpower programs.[48]

In Los Angeles, EEA was administered through its traditional organizational structure. The general manager of the personnel department maintained administrative responsibility and the program was implemented by the department's Employment Opportunities Division. The decision to administer EEA through the personnel department had important implications. City officials' view was

that the Act was providing funds to employ persons in the normal government functions, and the program should be looked upon as providing a supplement to the city budget rather than as a special manpower program, even though the funds were to be directed to hiring the unemployed.[49]

Allocation of Jobs

In distributing the jobs to agencies in New York City, consideration was given to the impact of the planned budget cuts in the 1971–1972 expense budget. More than 19,000 city jobs were cut for the fiscal year. Under EEA, New York City was allocated $15.8 million under Section 5, and $7.6 million under Section 6. This amount was minimal compared to other areas, considering the high rate of unemployment.[50]

It was decided that the board of education, the Health and Hospitals Corporation, and the police department would receive the highest priority under EEA. In anticipation of lay-offs of 3,500 teachers' jobs in the coming year, New York City decided to stress the board of education as a major target. These teacher positions, almost 30 percent of the total of all EEA Section 5 jobs, reflects a large number of professional slots in all of the data on

EEA in New York City.[51] A review of the participants in New York City suggests this strong inclination to recruit people with a high degree of education.[52]

In Chicago, the board of education and the Park District were brought in as subagents. The priority order of allocation of jobs was to education, which got the most slots, streets and sanitation, and then police.[53]

Milwaukee's Civil Service Commission contacted city departments to determine the distribution of EEA funds. They gave special focus on those projects that had been denied city funds previously. Public works received the largest number of slots, followed by city development and the school board.[54]

In Los Angeles, EEA officials allocated jobs among most departments with a stronger focus on jobs in some departments where there was a heavy demand for public services. Skill qualifications for most of the jobs were relatively low. Only the teachers, which comprised 9.6 percent of the jobs, required a college degree, and only the police officer positions, which comprised 5.9 percent of the jobs, required a high school diploma.[55]

Target Population

An important focus of the Emergency Employment Act was the goal to meet employment needs of the structurally unemployed. Although similarities of this group were illustrated in the act, and priority given to Vietnam veterans and heads of households, it was hoped that each city would address its distinct unemployment situation.[56]

In accordance with the Labor Department guidelines for EEA, New York City targeted three groups for hiring. It gave first priority to veterans who served in Indochina or Korea after August 5, 1964, and planned on recruiting 50 percent of the nonprofessional jobs developed from this group. The second highest priority was heads of households, and New York City expected that a minimum of 30 percent of the jobs would be filled by this group. A little under 30 percent of the jobs under Section 5 went to heads of households. The unemployed had priority over the underemployed for the remaining 20 percent of the jobs.[57]

It appears in New York City, however, that the major target

population goals were barely met, and little effort was made to hire from these groups. The city fell far short of its stated goals in the recruitment of Vietnam veterans. With regard to emphasis in the target population of those younger than twenty-two and older than forty-four, New York City seemed not to consider age a factor in planning, since 73 percent of the individuals hired were between the ages of twenty-two and forty-four.[58]

In Chicago, statistics demonstrated that the EEA program did reach many in the target population. More than 63 percent of the participants in Section 5 were minority group members, and more than 84 percent of the participants in Section 6 were from a minority group. In addition, more than 50 percent of the hirees were veterans. If one examines the educational profile, however, it appears that many of the participants who were reported as disadvantaged may have been liberally classified as such by Chicago. Therefore, employment of the hard-core unemployed was likely to be less than the figures given.[59]

In Milwaukee, background data of the enrollees indicate that program goals were met to varying degrees. Twenty-five percent of the enrollees had not attained a high school diploma, and 13 percent of the program enrollees had completed college. The small percentage of individuals with college degrees indicates Milwaukee's deemphasis on professional jobs for the program.[60]

Because hiring of veterans who had served since 1964 was particularly stressed, an overwhelming 69 percent of the program enrollees were between the ages of twenty-two and forty-four, and 18 percent were from the twenty-one-or-under age group. In addition, although 17 percent of the hirees were disadvantaged, Milwaukee did not view EEA as being primarily for the hard-core unemployed.[61]

Findings indicate that almost half of the participants were minority group members. These figures are particularly significant since blacks were represented in the EEA program by three times their numbers living in Milwaukee. Minority participation contrasted to the 9 percent of the city employees who were minority group members. According to city staff, they were recruited in their role as returning veterans rather than from a "disadvantaged" or "minority group."[62]

Information available on the background of program participants in Los Angeles indicates that most participants were in the twenty-two-to-forty-four year age group (70 percent), and that 85 percent had at least a high school education. A summary of the participants in June 1972 reflects a 56 percent representation by blacks, Chicanos, and Orientals; this compares with the same groups represented by 41 percent of the total Los Angeles population and about 45 percent of the unemployed at that time.[63]

Civil Service Requirements

In New York City the job descriptions for EEA positions were closely aligned to the requirements for regular civil service positions. City personnel department staff pressed for these classifications and requirements for the jobs because they would lend themselves easily to transition to regular, permanent positions in the civil service.[64]

This plan, however, was not necessarily compatible with recruitment from target populations. The policy committee in New York City chose to appoint EEA hirees under provisional status. If they had designated the program titles with temporary status rather than provisional status, the candidates would not have been required to meet regular civil service requirements. Civil service law in New York State requires provisional employees to meet the same qualifications as regular civil service employees. Boston chose to follow the temporary route.[65]

The fact that provisional status requires the same qualifications as regular civil service positions hindered the recruitment of individuals from the target groups, particularly the hard-core unemployed. Because most of the slots under Section 5 were for professional or skilled workers, the difficulty which the city had in meeting its quotas for Vietnam veterans and hard-core unemployed becomes evident.[66]

In contrast to New York City, Chicago has a looser civil service system which allows provisional appointments for indefinite periods; Chicago's civil service system did not create significant obstacles in recruiting for the EEA program. While Milwaukee's civil service system is elaborate, its formal education requirements are not as rigid as that of New York; therefore, Milwaukee was able to recruit from the target populations more easily.[67] Los Angeles hired 60 percent of the enrollees on an "emergency" basis. This qualified them as temporary employees until they passed the civil service examination. The only adjustment to the civil service which this required was to allow the EEA hirees to take the examination first, and if successful obtain certification and permanent appointment before "outside" candidates could take the test.[68]

Unions and Civil Service Employment

Labor unions were an important factor in implementation of the Emergency Employment Act throughout the country. In cities which have the strongest unions, obviously the impact was the most significant. Since New York City has some of the strongest municipal labor unions in the country, one can assume that these unions would get involved in the hiring of approximately 3,000 employees. These persons would be expected to meet regular civil service requirements. The unions were involved in the planning stages of EEA and successfully negotiated approximately one-third of the jobs allocated to agencies other than the board of education; the United Federation of Teachers influenced the allocation of slots for teachers. The unions also contested the appointment of individuals into positions where they felt regular civil service employees could be promoted.[69]

In Chicago, where Mayor Daley usually dealt with unions on an informal basis rather than through collective bargaining, and where the patronage system has long been the source of many city jobs, the unions did not exert significant influence. Milwaukee, which has nineteen separate municipal unions, adopted a cooperative approach to EEA. They were concerned about rehiring procedures, and satisfactory arrangements were made.[70]

A Temple University study of EEA in Detroit observes that unions in that city are usually strong and politically influential. There are 42 local unions representing municipal employees, so that one can assume that Detroit would anticipate union interests in developing plans for EEA. As a result they allocated most of the slots to entry-level positions. The American Federation of

State, County and Municipal Employees (AFSCME) local was concerned that EEA participants might receive preferential treatment. During the existence of the program, the AFSCME used established grievance procedures and won several cases involving bids by regular employees to obtain above-entry EEA jobs.[71]

Due to the city's fiscal crisis and civil service red tape in examinations, the Detroit EEA program got started quite slowly. Detroit, however, was able to satisfy the concerns of the unions due to the existing compatibility of union leaders and city officials.[72]

It would appear that the relationship between cities and unions in EEA implementation is an outgrowth of the existing political situation, and the situation of course would vary from city to city. The same would be true of civil service systems and their ability to adapt to the new program.[73]

Transition into Permanent Positions

If one evaluates EEA in New York City by the federal goal to move transitional employees into permanent civil service positions, then the city did poorly. At the end of August 1972, of the 4,130 cumulative participants, a total of 286 were placed in public jobs. Most were already on the civil service waiting list and more than half were teachers.[74]

Chicago was somewhat embarrassed by the meager number of EEA participants—about twenty—who made the transition to permanent jobs in the city. After one year of operation, the city had neither completed a listing of successful transfers to permanent jobs nor identified those participants who took or passed the examinations in job titles they were holding.[75]

In Milwaukee, as well, those EEA participants who made the transition to permanent employment were small in number. Thirty-nine workers in Section 6 made the transition to permanent jobs through October 1972, and 29 participants under Section 5 moved to permanent jobs.[76]

Data reflecting EEA participant transition to permanent jobs in Los Angeles at the end of the first year illustrates that 654 participants (12 percent of the total and 21 percent of the originally authorized positions) had obtained permanent jobs.[77] Los

Angeles seemed to take seriously the goal of EEA to place participants in permanent positions.

Conclusions

In accordance with the Emergency Employment Act of 1971, the federal government expected that institutions to whom funding was made available would analyze job descriptions and reevaluate skill requirements at all job levels, including civil service requirements and practices, "and the identification and elimination of artificial barriers to employment and occupational advancement of the disadvantaged."[78] These expectations, however, were unrealistic, given the limitations of the program and the role of municipal employee unions and professional organizations. Groups that oppose reform in civil service regulations (in New York City, for example) are highly influential, powerful figures in city politics. City personnel departments and municipal employee unions reject such change in an effort to protect their own constituencies. So long as jobs were temporary, unions and personnel professionals agreed on the goals of the program. But once it appeared that these goals could interfere with the mobility of existing constituencies in civil service, these groups were no longer cooperative.

There is no indication that any changes were made in civil service regulations in New York City that could be interpreted as an attempt at making it easier for EEA candidates to obtain civil service jobs. In fact, there was no evidence that the department of personnel undertook the analysis of job descriptions mandated in the legislation.[79]

Other EEA experiences across the country suggest, as in New York City, little or no institutional change. The Los Angeles experience showed the most potential for institutional change. This could be the result of support for change by a representative advisory board.[80]

What is important concerning the Emergency Employment Act as a model for public employment programs is that municipalities have little difficulty in spending funds and recruiting and hiring personnel. Of major concern, however, even when program agents reach target populations, is whether cities are capable of effectuating the transition of employees hired under public employment programs from temporary to permanent jobs.[81] A major barrier to implementing the transition is rigid civil service requirements. Cities need to be willing to make the necessary institutional changes in civil service.

THE COMPREHENSIVE EMPLOYMENT AND TRAINING ACT OF 1973

Like its predecessor, the Emergency Employment Act of 1971, the Comprehensive Employment and Training Act of 1973[82] (CETA) followed the model of the Works Progress Administration in its intent to provide jobs in a time of high unemployment. CETA was revised several times through the addition of various amendments, but its basic intent remained constant.

Because the primary focus of this study is on municipal civil service, this section concerning CETA will deal mostly with the Titles of the Act relating to Public Service Employment (PSE) and its attempt to combat structural unemployment by increasing access to civil service jobs. The PSE program had three main goals: (1) to provide jobs in a time of high unemployment; (2) to give employment experience to the structurally unemployed, thereby increasing their long-term job opportunities; and (3) to assist local governments in providing needed services. Congress did not specify priorities for each of the goals of the program. Consequently, the emphasis has shifted as economic and political conditions changed. Because PSE was highly decentralized, it changed in different ways in different areas as well. More than 450 state and local government units received PSE funds and distributed it to government and nonprofit agencies that employed PSE workers.[83]

Planning and Implementation

It was the intention of Congress and the Nixon administration to implement CETA quickly, and it appears that this goal was fulfilled, since the program was designed and participants hired within nine months of the passage of the act. Extensive planning was required to implement an effective transition from existing programs authorized by the Manpower Development and Training Act and the Economic Opportunity Act, which would expire on July 1, 1974.[84]

States, cities, counties, and consortia began implementing CETA. These prime sponsors, many of whom had little manpower program experience, started extensive preparation and began enrolling participants.[85]

The shift from categorical programs to a decentralized system was not simple. Prime sponsors at the state and local levels were involved in disentangling federal regulations and guidelines. This was all further complicated by the dramatic increase in unemployment in the fall of 1974.[86]

Many of the larger prime sponsors had administrative units assigned to their local government structure that had responsibility for manpower programs prior to CETA. Smaller municipalities needed to establish appropriate administrative apparatus. A Department of Labor evaluation study reports that 70 percent of the sponsors established the CETA unit either in the chief elected official's office or in an agency close to the chief elected official. The Labor Department study also suggests that staffing the new CETA units was difficult, inasmuch as staffs were limited in size and slowed by the inflexibility of civil service systems.[87]

Different prime sponsors used PSE differently. Some municipalities utilized PSE to fill essential jobs. In Detroit, for example, 19 percent of the sanitation workers and 10 percent of its police force were PSE enrollees in 1977. In 1978, about 25 percent of the convention center staff and 12 percent of the firefighters in Kansas City were PSE workers. In some governments, particularly in the South and West, PSE jobs may have been the only social services available to the poor. What is significant to note in the implementation stage is that the PSE guidelines were fairly broad.[88]

Allocation of Jobs

Local governments had relative discretion in choosing which agencies would employ PSE workers. While the 1978 Amendments curtailed flexibility in program administration by adding stricter monitoring and auditing provisions, the allocation of jobs to agencies remained a local decision. It is important to examine the agency selection process in order to determine program effectiveness.[89]

Studies indicate that most prime sponsors developed jobs within existing bureaucratic structures with relative ease. The recession had necessitated the curtailment of basic services, which local governments were glad to reinstate. Furthermore, there were added services which governments wished to provide that had long been beyond fiscal capability.[90] It should be noted, however, that inflexible civil service requirements often prevented prime sponsors from hiring persons from the target populations.

An evaluation of PSE notes that local governments, in effect, identified their objectives for the PSE program by the method they selected to allocate PSE slots to agencies.[91] It was reported that, in the criteria used to allocate jobs, certain governments stressed creating low-skill and low-wage jobs for PSE workers. In other cases, the nature of public services provided was more important.[92]

In general, it appears that local governments allocated jobs to agencies which best fit the determined objectives for the program. The allocation of jobs to nonprofit agencies is of particular importance. Federal and local officials play an important role in determining that their objectives are met by the variety of nonprofit organizations selected to receive PSE slots.[93]

Target Population

The basic objective of the PSE program was to provide jobs for the unemployed and the structurally unemployed in society. In attempting to achieve this goal, Congress periodically directed tightening of requirements for participant eligibility. PSE legislation, as written in Title II of the 1973 Act, required that participants had to be unemployed or underemployed when they became a PSE worker.[94] These requirements, however, did not prove especially restrictive.

Thus, one of the objectives of the 1978 CETA Amendments was to target Public Service Employment more narrowly to disadvantaged persons in the job market. After 1978, representation by minorities, women, youth, and poorly educated persons in PSE jobs increased. More than 90 percent of the PSE enrollees were economically disadvantaged.[95] It is worthy of note that while the minority and female representation in PSE positions increased after 1978, this was due primarily to stricter requirements on duration of unemployment than any assertion of federal regulations on affirmative action in CETA.

Following the 1978 Amendments, the PSE program appeared to be hiring persons with other characteristics that made them structurally unemployable. For example, new enrollees with less than a high school education increased from 25 percent in 1978 to 35 percent in 1980. PSE workers who were members of a minority group increased from 39 percent in 1978 to 48 percent in 1980, and new enrollees who were female increased from 38 percent in 1978 to 46 percent in 1980.[96]

In analyzing the change in participants' characteristics as a result of the 1978 Amendments, one study observes that targeting alone is not adequate for the success of PSE as a model for hiring the structurally unemployed. Success is also highly dependent on meeting training and transition goals.[97]

Civil Service Requirements

It appears that inflexible civil service requirements restricted PSE program activities in large cities, as it had its predecessor, the EEA. An evaluation of the program observes that in some cities the entry-level salaries for certain job categories in civil service were higher than the salary permitted under PSE.[98]

As with EEA, other barriers, such as difficulty with the PSE target population meeting minimum civil service qualifications and required examinations, impeded PSE implementation. Civil service rules, regulations, and classification systems, which have developed long histories, are often supported by workers and civil service personnel professionals who resist any change in the system. While attempts have been made at adjusting civil service systems, for the most part it is the PSE program that was required to fit into the existing system.[99]

The impact of unions and civil service systems on PSE seemed greater in large cities since the rules were more deeply entrenched over a longer period of time. Public employee unions also had greater influence in large cities, especially in the East.[100]

Unions and Civil Service Employment

Public employee unions had an impact on PSE. According to the legislation, unions had the opportunity to comment on prime sponsor's plans. Some unions suggested that the role given to them was too limited, or that the time allowed to review the plans was insufficient. In certain instances labor pressed for increased representation on the planning council. The main focus of their concerns, however, was twofold: "(a) protecting the wage and employment conditions of the regular employees in government and private industry, and (b) ensuring that the employment and training design and operation would enhance the employability of CETA participants."[101]

The limits on the PSE allowable wages were designed to recruit unskilled persons rather than those who might be able to find unsubsidized jobs and to limit the creation of high-paying jobs in order to discourage local governments from replacing regular employees with PSE enrollees. While prime sponsors may have reached their target populations through these restrictions, they became controversial issues for public employee unions and civil service commissions. A prime issue for PSE was the extent to which municipal employee unions and civil service systems dealt with the lower salary scale of PSE jobs.[102]

One study reported that wage restrictions were causing problems in approximately half of the jurisdictions they studied. Problems were the greatest where union opposition to wage restrictions was the strongest. They report that, in one large city, union opposition to job restructuring was so strong that the city did not attempt any.[103]

In the other half of the governments studied, wage restrictions did not appear to be a significant problem. This was due primarily to the fact that these prime sponsors were in southern and rural areas where active unions or high civil service salaries do not exist. Several of these localities were able to establish special civil service job classifications.[104]

While conflict between unions and local governments is apparent with regard to PSE, compromise was reached in several large cities with strong unions.[105] As long as public employee unions, however, perceive that low-wage employees are performing the same tasks as regular workers it appears that they will view such public employment programs as a threat.

Transition into Permanent Positions

Finding permanent, unsubsidized jobs for the participants has long been a goal of public employment programs. This was also the goal of CETA. Thus, CETA's success must be evaluated by the number of participants who obtained unsubsidized employment and their earnings. The kinds of preparation and training participants receive significantly affects their chances for unsubsidized jobs.[106]

A summary of data from prime sponsors in a CETA study indicates that about one-third of all PSE enrollees were placed in jobs upon termination. They indicate, however, that the figures are underreported and that the numbers of placements increased over time. The research also indicates that 55 percent of those PSE enrollees who started the program in 1976 and worked for three to fifteen months were employed one month after termination. Research further shows that PSE enrollees had difficulty in finding suitable jobs, especially in the distressed large cities, when they terminated PSE jobs.[107]

It appears, however, that some prime sponsors which were observed in a Brookings study did make exerted efforts to meet transition goals. But, often, lack of connections in the private sector, failure by participants to pass civil service examinations, or lack of jobs in the region prevented sponsors from achieving their objectives.[108]

Conclusions

It may be worthwhile noting a few observations concerning PSE. Some of the provisions in the 1978 Amendments were antithetical to the principles of civil service systems and public employee unions. Wage restrictions, for example, pose implementation difficulties for local officials in some governments. What was significant is whether prime sponsors made special efforts to encourage municipal unions and civil service systems to adjust to these restrictions, or ignored the federal guidelines.[109]

CONCLUSIONS

It becomes evident through the programs (Paraprofessionals, EEA, and CETA) examined in this chapter that the evaluation of public employment programs is a complicated, multifaceted problem, which requires analysis on several levels. Evaluation of congressional intent, the relationship between policy objectives and administrative procedure and response, and the realization of program objectives must be addressed.

Thus, examination of the public employment programs in this chapter indicates that, while there have been some advances, for the most part these programs have not had a major impact on changing municipal civil service systems to make them more open, less exclusionary structures with a greater degree of social equity. In order to be effective, public employment programs must devise legislation geared toward changing inflexible civil service systems, which discourage the recruitment of the structurally unemployed. The legislation analyzed in this chapter provides for only limited guarantees that artificial barriers will be replaced by open access systems of government employment. None of the legislation, however, requires governments to reduce credentialling requirements or to provide encouragement to restructure civil service systems.[110]

To assume that additional funding or new public employment programs such as EEA or CETA would bring relief to the structurally unemployed is to ignore the basic deficiencies in civil service systems, that is, their lack of flexibility.

NOTES

1. Marilyn Gittell, "Public Employment and the Public Service," in *Public Service Employment: An Analysis of Its History, Problems, and*

Prospects, ed. Alan Gartner, Russell A. Nixon, and Frank Riessman (New York: Praeger Publishers, 1973), pp. 121, 141.

2. Helen Ginsburg, *Unemployment, Subemployment, and Public Policy* (New York: Center for Studies in Income Maintenance Policy, New York University School of Social Work, 1975), pp. 2–3.

3. Frances Fox Piven and Richard A. Cloward, *Regulating the Poor: The Functions of Public Welfare* (New York: Pantheon Books, 1971), p. 68.

4. Ibid., p. 69.

5. Ibid., p. 74.

6. Ibid., p. 94.

7. "Jobs in the Great Depression," *New York Times*, 22 December 1974, sec. 1, p. 1.

8. The agency was renamed the Work Projects Administration in July 1939; Piven and Cloward, *Regulating the Poor*, p. 96.

9. Sar A. Levitan, "Does Public Job Creation Offer Any Hope?" *The Conference Board RECORD* 12 (August 1975): 58; Robert Lekachman, *Public Service Employment: Jobs for All* (New York: Public Affairs Pamphlets, 1972), p. 10.

10. Lekachman, *Public Service Employment*, p. 10.

11. Arthur MacMahon, John Millet, and Gladys Ogden, *The Administration of Federal Work Relief* (Chicago: Public Administration Service, 1941).

12. Ibid.

13. Ibid., p. 207.

14. Ibid.

15. Donald S. Howard, *The WPA and Federal Relief Policy* (New York: Russell Sage Foundation, 1943), p. 288.

16. Piven and Cloward, *Regulating the Poor*, p. 98.

17. Helen Ginsburg, *Unemployment or Full Employment?* (New York: Center for Studies in Income Maintenance Policy, New York University School of Social Work, 1975), p. 7.

18. Ibid., pp. 7–8.

19. Russell A. Nixon, "The Historical Development of the Conception and Implementation of Full Employment as Economic Policy," in *Public Service Employment: An Analysis of Its History, Problems, and Prospects*, ed. Alan Gartner, Russell A. Nixon, and Frank Riessman (New York: Praeger Publishers, 1973), pp. 26–37; for further discussion of full employment policy see Stanley Moses, ed., "Planning for Full Employment," *The Annals of the American Academy of Political and Social Science* 418 (March 1975): ix–164.

20. Ginsburg, *Unemployment or Full Employment?* p. 8.

21. Piven and Cloward, *Regulating the Poor*, p. 261.

22. Ibid., p. 263.

23. Alan Gartner, Vivian Carter Jackson, and Frank Riessman, eds., *Paraprofessionals in Education Today* (New York: Human Sciences Press, 1977), p. 4; for a discussion of the role of paraprofessionals in human services improvement, see Alan Gartner, *Paraprofessionals and Their Performance: A Survey of Education, Health, and Social Service Programs* (New York: Praeger Publishers, 1971).

24. This section utilizes a series of interviews conducted with a representative number of teacher and health paraprofessionals and program administrators in New York City; the material was part of an unpublished manpower study conducted at the Institute for Community Studies, Queens College, C.U.N.Y., 1974.

25. *Congressional Quarterly (CQ) Weekly Report No. 29 Part 2*, 22 July 1966, vol. 24, p. 1595.

26. Arthur Pearl and Frank Riessman, *New Careers for the Poor: The Non-Professional in Human Service* (New York: The Free Press, 1965); see also Frank Riessman and Hermine I. Popper, *Up From Poverty: New Career Ladders for Nonprofessionals* (New York: Harper & Row, 1968).

27. *Congressional Quarterly*, pp. 1595–1596.

28. "Manual for Utilization of Auxiliary Personnel" (New York: Board of Education, Auxiliary Educational Career Unit, 1967–1970), p. 13.

29. "Paraprofessionals: Criteria for Eligibility," Bronx River Education Action Committee, Bronx, N.Y., 1967.

30. See New York City Commission on Human Rights, *The Employment of Minorities, Women and the Handicapped in City Government: A Report of a 1971 Survey*, September 1973, p. 33.

31. *Agreement between the Board of Education of the City School District of the City of New York and United Federation of Teachers, Local 2, American Federation of Teachers, AFL-CIO covering Teacher Aide, Educational Assistant, Educational Associate, Auxiliary Trainer, Bi-Lingual Professional Assistant*, 9 September 1982–9 September 1984.

32. In establishing selection criteria, the Bronx Maternity and Guidance Center Community Board established the high school diploma criterion for selection of externs due to the extensive training period in anatomy, biology, and physiology.

33. For a discussion of the development of paraprofessionals in education for handicapped children, pre-school programs, reading programs, and guidance programs, see Gartner, Jackson, and Riessman, *Paraprofessionals in Education Today*.

34. "New Directions," *The Newsletter of the National Resource Center*

for Paraprofessionals in Special Education, New Careers Training Laboratory, City University of New York, vol. 4, no. 1, Winter 1983.

35. Pearl and Riessman, *New Careers for the Poor*.

36. U.S. Congress, *Emergency Employment Act of 1971*, Pub. L. 92–54, 92nd Cong., 12 July 1971.

37. Sar A. Levitan and Robert Taggart, "Summary Report I: An Overview," in *Emergency Employment Act: The PEP Generation*, ed. Sar A. Levitan and Robert Taggart (Salt Lake City, Utah: Olympus Publishing Company, 1974), p. 11.

38. Marilyn Gittell, "Putting Merit Back in the Merit System" *Social Policy* 3 (September/October 1972): 23–24.

39. Marilyn Gittell, "Summary Report IX: New York City," in *Emergency Employment Act: The PEP Generation*, ed. Sar A. Levitan and Robert Taggart (Salt Lake City, Utah: Olympus Publishing Company, 1974), pp. 201–202.

40. Howard W. Hallman, *Emergency Employment: A Study in Federalism* (University, Ala.: The University of Alabama Press, 1977), p. 47.

41. See U.S. Senate, Committee on Labor and Public Welfare, *Case Studies of the Emergency Employment Act in Operation* (1973) for an extensive evaluation of EEA in several large cities.

42. Hallman, *Emergency Employment*, p. 71.

43. Gittell, "Summary Report IX: New York City," p. 202.

44. Ibid.

45. Marilyn Gittell, "Evaluation of the Implementation of the Emergency Employment Act in New York City," Prepared for the National Manpower Task Force, October 1972, pp. 5–8. (Mimeographed.)

46. Ibid.

47. Hallman, *Emergency Employment*, p. 72.

48. Ibid.

49. Walter Fogel, "Summary Report VI: Los Angeles City and County," in *Emergency Employment Act: The PEP Generation*, ed. Sar A. Levitan and Robert Taggart (Salt Lake City, Utah: Olympus Publishing Company, 1974), p. 137.

50. Gittell, "Summary Report IX: New York City," pp. 203–204.

51. Gittell, "Evaluation of the Implementation of the Emergency Employment Act in New York City," p. 14.

52. Gittell, "Summary Report IX: New York City," p. 204.

53. Hallman, *Emergency Employment*, pp. 74–75.

54. Ibid., p. 75.

55. Fogel, "Summary Report VI: Los Angeles City and County," pp. 138–140.

56. Gittell, "Summary Report IX: New York City," p. 207.

57. Ibid.

58. Ibid., pp. 209–210.

59. Myron Roomkin, "Summary Report II: Chicago," in *Emergency Employment Act: The PEP Generation*, ed. Sar A. Levitan and Robert Taggart (Salt Lake City, Utah: Olympus Publishing Company, 1974), pp. 69–70.

60. Peter Kobrak, "Summary Report VIII: Milwaukee," in *Emergency Employment Act: The PEP Generation*, ed. Sar A. Levitan and Robert Taggart (Salt Lake City, Utah: Olympus Publishing Company, 1974), p. 189.

61. Ibid.

62. Ibid., p. 190.

63. Fogel, "Summary Report VI: Los Angeles City and County," pp. 144–145.

64. Gittell, "Summary Report IX: New York City," p. 212.

65. Ibid.

66. Ibid.

67. Hallman, *Emergency Employment*, p. 113.

68. Fogel, "Summary Report VI: Los Angeles City and County," pp. 141–142.

69. Gittell, "Summary Report IX: New York City," p. 213.

70. Hallman, *Emergency Employment*, pp. 77–78, 118–119.

71. Ibid., pp. 119–120.

72. Ibid., p. 120.

73. Hallman, *Emergency Employment*, p. 123.

74. Gittell, "Summary Report IX: New York City," p. 218.

75. Roomkin, "Summary Report II: Chicago," pp. 71–72.

76. Kobrak, "Summary Report VIII: Milwaukee," pp. 194–195.

77. Fogel, "Summary Report VI: Los Angeles City and County," p. 146.

78. Gittell, "Summary Report IX: New York City," p. 217.

79. Ibid., pp. 217–218.

80. Gittell, "Public Employment and the Public Service," p. 135.

81. Gittell, "Summary Report IX: New York City," p. 220.

82. U.S. Congress, *Comprehensive Employment and Training Act of 1973*, Pub. L. 93–203, 93rd Cong., 28 December 1973.

83. Richard P. Nathan et al., *Public Service Employment: A Field Evaluation* (Washington, D.C.: The Brookings Institution, 1981), pp. 1–2.

84. Bonnie B. Snedeker and David M. Snedeker, *CETA: Decentralization on Trial* (Salt Lake City, Utah: Olympus Publishing Company, 1978), pp. 33–34.

85. Ibid., p. 34.

86. Ibid.

87. Ibid., pp. 52–53.

88. Janet M. Galchick, "Administering Public Service Employment: The Effects of the 1978 CETA Amendments," paper presented at the meeting of the American Society for Public Administration, Detroit, April 1981, pp. 1–2.

89. Galchick, "Administering Public Service Employment," pp. 5–6; for an analysis of the allocation of PSE jobs before the 1978 Amendments, see William Mirengoff and Lester Rindler, *CETA: Manpower Programs Under Local Control* (Washington, D.C.: National Academy of Sciences, 1978).

90. Snedeker and Snedeker, *CETA: Decentralization on Trial*, p. 227.

91. Robert F. Cook et al., *Public Service Employment in Fiscal Year 1980* (Princeton, N.J.: Princeton Urban and Regional Research Center, Princeton University, March 1981), p. 23. (Unpublished material.)

92. Ibid., p. 24.

93. Ibid., p. 25.

94. Richard P. Nathan et al., *Monitoring the Public Service Employment Program: The Second Round* (Washington, D.C.: National Commission for Employment Policy, 1979), p. 81.

95. William Mirengoff et al., *CETA: Accomplishments Problems Solutions* (Kalamazoo, Mich.: W. E. Upjohn Institute for Employment Research, 1982), p. 107.

96. Ibid., p. 115.

97. Cook et al., *Public Service Employment in Fiscal Year 1980*, pp. 55, 57.

98. Nathan et al., *Public Service Employment*, p. 80.

99. Ibid., p. 81.

100. Ibid.

101. Mirengoff et al., *CETA: Accomplishments Problems Solutions*, p. 237.

102. Galchick, "Administering Public Service Employment," p. 19.

103. Ibid., pp. 19–20.

104. Ibid., p. 20.

105. Nathan et al., *Public Service Employment*, p. 78.

106. Mirengoff et al., *CETA: Accomplishments Problems Solutions*, p. 267.

107. Cook et al., *Public Service Employment in Fiscal Year 1980*, p. 73.

108. Nathan et al., *Public Service Employment*, p. 53.

109. Galchick, "Administering Public Service Employment," p. 31.

110. Gittell, "Public Employment and the Public Service," p. 141.

Conclusions   6

PROBLEM BACKGROUND

The purpose of this study was to examine the hypothesis that
the rigid structure of municipal civil service systems and the
principle of meritocracy underlying that system have contributed
to and maintained a system of social inequity in the public service, and that such values as representation and responsive service delivery are secondary to the protection of professional
power and control.

Even though the public service does provide large numbers
of jobs for minorities and women, the numbers of jobs are insufficient, as compared to their representation in the general
population. The research in this study concludes that minorities
and women have been at a competitive disadvantage in public
employment in the United States. While the total number of
minorities and women have increased in the government workforce, they have not attained representative levels in the high-
ranking, better status, and better paying positions within civil
service. Minorities often tend to be clustered in service, maintenance, and paraprofessional jobs, and women are frequently

overrepresented in clerical positions. The public service has had an exclusionary effect on minorities and women.

The public service has been one of the fastest growing sectors of the employment market, particularly at the state and local government levels. While it may be argued that the public service should offer the greatest opportunity for entrance of minority populations into the economic system, this has not been the case. The major reason for this can be attributed to the rigid structure of the civil service system.

The civil service (or merit) system was created both to ensure the selection of competent individuals and prevent the use of patronage in gaining political influence. The merit system was an outgrowth of the "good government" movement and was characterized by selection devices based on competitive examinations, relative security of tenure and political neutrality. Once appointed to such a position in the public service an individual could assume tenure until retirement. Civil service supporters believed that these procedures would guarantee recruitment on the basis of objective measures of competence.

What was significant under the merit system, particularly as it developed its own procedures and screening devices, was that only those who had achieved a certain level of education were eligible for jobs. What emerged was a theory and practice of meritocracy that assumed that the best candidates were those who were most literate and most learned. In contrast, the patronage system encompassed recruitment procedures which allowed for a cross-section of the population to enter public service without regard to level of education achieved.[1]

As discussed in this study, if one analyzes the goals of the civil service reformers, against their achievements their considerable success becomes evident. The introduction of merit principles added some measure of business efficiency as well as removing the spoils. It has been suggested that the reformers were displaced patricians trying to regain political power from the *nouveau riche* and the immigrant-supported machines.[2] The leadership in civil service reform associations was composed mainly of professionals, such as editors, lawyers, doctors, clergymen, and professors who came from families in society of established wealth.[3]

What is significant is the attempt by these businessmen and professionals to shift the locus of power from a decentralized ward system, representative in municipal affairs of lower- and middle-class interests, to a more expansive scope of city affairs in which their own conception of public policy could dominate.[4] While civil service reform did not return the patrician to power, it did start to destroy the immigrant machines and the ability of the *nouveau riche* to buy political power.

Proponents of the merit system claimed that employees hired according to merit principles would make the bureaucracy more representative of the general population. They argued that the openness of the civil service, the ability of individuals at the lower levels of society to elevate their status, while simultaneously representing variety, was a major benefit of the merit system.[5] The merit system, however, did not prove to be an "open" system. The principle of social equity was abandoned under the merit system for the concept of "neutral competence," whereby individuals who were not prepared to perform competent work within the public service were screened out by supposedly neutral standards.

Only those who had achieved a certain level of education, possessed credentials, and could pass examinations were eligible for jobs under the merit system. These factors combined with vested interests developed by personnel departments, professional organizations, and municipal unions to maintain the status quo have had an exclusionary effect on the attempt by newer groups to achieve similar status in civil service, as compared with older immigrant groups under the patronage system.

IMPACT OF MUNICIPAL CIVIL SERVICE SYSTEMS

Practices and procedures in municipal civil service systems have a significant impact on the ability of minorities and women to compete for jobs within merit systems. If attempts are made at eliminating discriminatory aspects of municipal civil service systems, it is essential to have an understanding of policy making in the current system. Personnel professionals, civil service commissions, professional organizations, and municipal unions all have an impact on the process. The selection devices within the merit system, including qualifications, examinations, and promotional requirements, which were an outgrowth of an attempt to reform government structure, have had an exclusionary effect on minority and female employment in the municipal government workforce. The essential feature of the merit system is the use of the written competitive examination as a selection device for determining qualification for appointment. Those who score the highest on the examination are considered the most qualified for the job.

There are those who believe that minorities, particularly blacks, are intellectually inferior and therefore do not achieve well on examinations.[6] This is an important allegation in view of the discussion that the examination system in municipal civil service systems has an exclusionary effect on the entrance and promotion of some minorities in civil service. The combination, however, of examinations which are often culturally biased, entrance requirements that are unrelated to job performance, and inflated education qualifications for lower-level positions are some of the reasons that the municipal civil service system has a discriminatory impact on minorities.

While women are represented by significant numbers in civil service jobs they are overrepresented in the low paying entry-level positions with limited career ladder opportunities. There are often structural differences between positions defined typically as "male" or "female." The entrance requirements for the female job categories are often higher and offer fewer career ladder opportunities.[7] Examinations and requirements, such as those set for uniformed services, have a discriminatory impact on women.

In examining the structure and role of the participants in civil service decision making it was noted that the first civil service commissions sprang up as a result of the civil service reform movement's desire to free the public servant from political influence and incorporate the principles of scientific management. The agency was usually bipartisan or nonpartisan in nature, and was designed to ensure that individuals entered the public service only through merit.

Change in personnel orientation from merit maintainers to personnel managers prompted the development of a more professionalized public service, one with increased credentials requirements, and the mechanism of public employee collective bargaining. These tools are at the very heart of a personnel management system and are often used against the interests of abstract merit principles and against the interests of an open civil service system.

Dependence on the professional worked directly against the interests of an open civil service system, because professionals, in order to maintain and enhance their financial and social status, favored a closed personnel system. By restricting entrance in the civil service only to those who met their own definition of a qualified applicant, the professionals were legitimizing their role as possessors of a unique and socially beneficial skill, thereby enhancing their own social and economic worth.

An open civil service system is important, not just in terms of promoting a government workforce representative of its numbers in the general population, but in better service delivery. Civil service systems are powerful institutions that make policy impacting the citizenry. When the ideologies and value structures perpetuated by the professional recruitment process run counter to the interests of the communities being served by these professionals, the results may be unsatisfactory. Although the potential conflict of professional interest versus community interest is always present, it is most acute when the communities in question are severely underrepresented in the professional ranks. In such cases, there is much less incentive on the part of the organization to adjust their services to fit the needs of the community and yet, ironically, more need for it to do so. It has been suggested that a democratic theory of administration needs to focus more on the responsiveness of administration to constituent service needs, in contrast to more traditional concepts of public administration.[8]

Collective bargaining has intensified the professionalization of municipal civil service systems by involvement in determining standards and requirements for civil service positions. The prevailing situation is that unions with the greatest impact on personnel policy are those who most strongly advocate a status quo, or what the author would characterize as a closed-door policy. Some researchers observe that those unions with the least power are those most amenable to fundamental changes in the personnel system. They often represent those in lower-level jobs with greater minority representation. The impact of collective bargaining on personnel activities in the interests of minorities is either minimal or negative.[9] Often the uniformed services unions present significant institutional barriers to minorities.[10]

This study has highlighted the compatibility of municipal union values with personnel department goals. These goals in maintaining a status quo, closed personnel system are not compatible with eliminating institutional barriers that affect the success of minorities in the civil service system and promoting more responsive service delivery systems.

Most mayors in large cities have not been particularly effective at eliminating the structural barriers in municipal civil service systems, which preclude easy access and promotion opportunities for minorities and women in civil service jobs. It appears, however, that in a few cities, such as Detroit and Atlanta, the black mayors were able to provide significant leadership in achieving affirmative action in civil service systems. Thus, despite existing civil service systems, it is possible for mayoral leadership to provide the impetus for such changes that would open civil service jobs to greater numbers of minorities.

It has been argued in this study that the civil service system was rationalized and developed to ensure fairness and equal access to government positions. The system, however, has not worked that way. The reason is that civil service institutions, which pretend to be neutral, are exclusionary. Among the major institutional barriers to full participation of minority and female groups in municipal civil service are the job classification, the credentialling requirements, and the examination process. It is clear that many things have worked against opening the system, and attempts at making civil service more open bring very strong resistance.

EFFORTS TO ACHIEVE SOCIAL EQUITY IN MUNICIPAL CIVIL SERVICE

This study has examined efforts to challenge the discriminatory aspects of municipal civil service systems and make the system more equitable. The purpose in doing so was to determine if change was feasible, who resisted, and why? These efforts include affirmative action programs, legal action, and public employment programs.

In examining efforts to achieve social equity in civil service systems, one must look at the development of the system and the various programs designed for that purpose. Many of these programs were created to recruit minority groups to the public service. They emerged in response to charges of discrimination in the regular civil service system and lack of responsiveness to service delivery needs of the community. Data indicated that, although the civil service served as an important source of minority employment, the number of minority people in such systems was minimal.

Inherent in the intent of affirmative action is the establishment of a representative bureaucracy. If the government workforce is representative of the general population of the city, it is believed that the government can better serve the needs and demands of the population.[11]

Various legal and legislative instruments exist which are the basis for reversing discrimination in civil service systems. They include the Fifth and Fourteenth Amendments to the Constitution, Title VII of the Civil Rights Act of 1964, and the Equal Employment Opportunity Act of 1972, which made the antidiscrimination provisions of Title VII applicable to local governments. The legislation, however, has not been remarkably effective.

Discrimination is prevalent in all aspects of personnel systems including the recruitment and selection process. A major issue pertaining to the selection process has been the lack of validity of examinations as they relate to race, sex, and ethnicity. There have been many court cases dealing with this question. Other practices which are alleged to be discriminatory include veterans' preference and seniority systems.

The intent of affirmative action plans is to increase minorities and females in the government workforce. The use of goals and quotas associated with affirmative action continues to be controversial. Some believe that progress is being made. There are those who oppose affirmative action programs, which are intended to correct alleged discrimination of minorities in public employment. There are those who argue against the use of any kind of quotas to remedy the exclusionary aspects of municipal civil service systems, as well as other institutions in society. These individuals believe that the use of quotas and goals will create a condition of reverse discrimination.[12] Still others argue that, despite legislative action and numerous court cases, little success has been achieved.[13]

Empirical data, however, can reveal the extent to which current civil service systems institutionally discriminate against minorities and women. City government bureaucracies were found to be the most representative of all levels of government. Minorities are represented to a greater extent in local government employment than some would have assumed. But again, they are overrepresented in the low-paying, less prestigious positions. Moreover, while women fill a high proportion of the low-paying jobs, they are less represented in comparison to their numbers in the general population than many would have believed.

As affirmative action programs and other efforts failed to effectively eliminate discriminatory aspects of civil service systems, legal action was viewed by some as a mechanism to challenge the system. This study examined several of the cases which challenged one particular aspect of civil service systems, the selection process.

Griggs v. Duke Power Company was a Supreme Court case involving testing procedures within a private company. It set a precedent for future cases involving employment selection devices which exclude proportionate numbers of minority group members. The Court held that Title VII of the Civil Rights Act of 1964 mandated that the burden of proof demonstrating the relevancy of job requirements to employment rests with the employer.

In the three other cases reviewed, *Chance v. Board of Examiners, Guardians Association of New York v. Civil Service Commission,* and *Berkman v. City of New York,* the courts dealt respectively with the selection of principals and other supervisory personnel in the New York City school system, the hiring of entry-level police officers and the promotion of sergeants in the New York City

Police Department, and the selection of firefighters in the New York City Fire Department.

The courts found, in these cases, the civil service examination procedures and selection devices to be unconstitutional insofar as they discriminate against minorities and women. In dealing with these inequities the courts have attempted to structure remedial action.

While judicial action has played a critical role in supporting social equity in the civil service system, it is important to focus on the resistance to implementation of its decisions. During the eight years in which an interim system was established to appoint principals in the New York City public schools, as a result of the court decision in *Chance v. Board of Examiners*, significant numbers of minorities were appointed to these supervisory positions. However, since this interim system expired and the board of examiners has regained responsibility for promulgating eligible lists, significantly fewer minorities have been appointed principals.

What is significant about this experience is that while the courts have established the legal failure of the system they have not been able to foster change. It will be important for future research to evaluate the results of these court decisions to determine their long-term impact on restructuring civil service systems.

The data collected for this study demonstrate municipal civil service to be closed systems. Both the government employment data and the court findings confirm this.

Several public employment programs were also evaluated in this study to determine their success in challenging the merit system. Since the Great Depression of the 1930s, the government has used public service employment as a device for hiring the chronically unemployed. These programs attempted to present structural alternatives to the normal civil service procedure in order to accomplish certain employment goals.

The study examined paraprofessional programs, the Emergency Employment Act of 1971 (EEA), and the Comprehensive Employment and Training Act of 1973 (CETA). These programs did very little to eliminate the artificial barriers in municipal civil service systems that exclude minorities. This should not be surprising, since none of the legislation creating these programs provided incentives to governments for reducing credentialling requirements or restructuring the rigid civil service systems.

This study has demonstrated that the rigid structure of municipal civil service systems and the principle of meritocracy underlying that system have contributed to and maintained a system of social inequity. Personnel professionals appear to have a greater stake in promoting the merit principles than in creating a personnel system open to all groups, improving delivery of services, and establishing a representative bureaucracy. While the civil service system was originally designed to produce quality and equity, it has accomplished neither.

Municipal civil service systems can provide great opportunities for the employment of minorities and women at responsible levels. Employment of these individuals can further serve to establish a representative bureaucracy. While the concept of representation is not simple, proponents would argue that a government workforce representative of the population would most likely get involved in pursuits of the public interest.[14]

The research in this study suggests that a shift in personnel practices which would facilitate a representative bureaucracy is a complex problem. Some of the constraints associated with the inability to make civil service more equitable have to do with broad concepts relating to power and jobs, racism, and sexism in American society.

NOTES

1. Paul P. Van Riper, *History of the United States Civil Service* (Evanston, Ill.: Row, Peterson and Company, 1958).

2. Ari Hoogenboom, *Outlawing the Spoils: A History of the Civil Service Reform Movement 1865–1883* (Urbana, Ill.: University of Illinois Press, 1961), pp. 179–197.

3. Ibid., pp. ix–x.

4. Samuel P. Hays, "The Politics of Reform in Municipal Government in the Progressive Era," in *Social Change and Urban Politics: Readings,* ed. Daniel N. Gordon (Englewood Cliffs, N.J.: Prentice-Hall, 1973), pp. 113–118.

5. Harold F. Gortner, *Administration in the Public Sector* (New York: John Wiley & Sons, 1977), p. 273.

6. For a discussion and refutation of this argument see Philip Green, *The Pursuit of Inequality* (New York: Pantheon Books, 1981).

7. Sandra Peterson-Hardt and Nancy D. Perlman, *Sex-Segregated Career Ladders in New York State Government: A Structural Analysis of Inequality in Employment* (Albany, N.Y.: Center for Women in Government, State University of New York at Albany, October 1979), pp. 1–3, 18, 82–83.

8. See Vincent Ostrom, *The Intellectual Crisis in American Public Administration* (University, Ala.: The University of Alabama Press, 1973), pp. 132–133.

9. Raymond D. Horton, *Municipal Labor Relations in New York City: Lessons of the Lindsay-Wagner Years* (New York: Praeger Publishers, 1972), pp. 112–113, 116.

10. William B. Gould, "Labor Relations and Race Relations," in *Public Workers and Public Unions*, ed. Sam Zagoria (Englewood Cliffs, N.J.: Prentice-Hall, 1972), pp. 156–157.

11. Gortner, *Administration in the Public Sector*, p. 293.

12. Nathan Glazer, *Affirmative Discrimination: Ethnic Inequality and Public Policy* (New York: Basic Books, 1975; Harper Colophon Books, 1978), pp. ix–xix.

13. Robert D. Lee, Jr., *Public Personnel Systems* (Baltimore: University Park Press, 1979), p. 280.

14. Hanna Fenichel Pitkin, *The Concept of Representation* (Berkeley, Calif.: University of California Press, 1967).

Selected Bibliography

BOOKS AND MONOGRAPHS

Appleby, Paul H. *Policy and Administration*. University, Ala.: University of Alabama Press, 1949.

Aronson, Sidney H. *Status and Kinship in the Higher Civil Service: Standards of Selection in the Administrations of John Adams, Thomas Jefferson and Andrew Jackson*. Cambridge, Mass.: Harvard University Press, 1964.

Bachrach, Peter. *The Theory of Democratic Elitism: A Critique*. Boston: Little, Brown and Company, 1967.

Baikie, Edith. *Civil Service in the City of New York: A Study of the Operations of the Municipal Civil Service Commission with Recommended Reforms*. New York: Citizens Budget Commission, 1938.

Banfield, Edward C. *Political Influence: A New Theory of Urban Politics*. New York: The Free Press, 1961.

Banfield, Edward C., and Wilson, James Q. *City Politics*. New York: Vintage Books, 1963.

Benson, George C. S. *The Administration of the Civil Service in Massachusetts: With Special Reference to State Control of City Civil Service*. Cambridge, Mass.: Harvard University Press, 1935.

Berg, Ivar. *Education and Jobs: The Great Training Robbery*. Boston: Beacon Press, 1971.

Bowles, Samuel, and Gintis, Herbert. *Schooling in Capitalist America: Educational Reform and the Contradictions of Economic Life.* New York: Basic Books, 1976.

Caro, Robert A. *The Power Broker: Robert Moses and the Fall of New York.* New York: Alfred A. Knopf, 1974.

Chaiken, Jan M., and Cohen, Bernard. *Police Civil Service Selection Procedures in New York City: Comparison of Ethnic Groups,* R–1289. New York: The New York City Rand Institute, May 1973.

Connery, Robert H. *Governmental Organization within the City of New York.* New York: Institute of Public Administration, 1960.

Cook, Ann; Gittell, Marilyn; and Mack, Herb, eds. *City Life, 1865–1900: Views of Urban America.* New York: Praeger Publishers, 1973.

Crossland, Fred E. *Minority Access to College: A Ford Foundation Report.* New York: Schocken Books, 1971.

Dahl, Robert A. *Who Governs? Democracy and Power in an American City.* New Haven: Yale University Press, 1961.

Dahlberg, Jane S. *The New York Bureau of Municipal Research: Pioneer in Government Administration.* New York: New York University Press, 1966.

David, Stephen M., and Peterson, Paul E., eds. *Urban Politics and Public Policy: The City in Crisis.* New York: Praeger Publishers, 1973.

Dobson, John M. *Politics in the Gilded Age: A New Perspective on Reform.* New York: Praeger Publishers, 1972.

Eisinger, Peter K. *Black Employment in City Government, 1973–1980.* Washington, D.C.: Joint Center for Political Studies, 1983.

Fogelson, Robert M. *The Fragmented Metropolis: Los Angeles 1850–1930.* Cambridge, Mass.: Harvard University Press, 1967.

Foulke, William Dudley. *Fighting the Spoilsmen.* New York: The Knickerbocker Press, 1919.

Franklin, Grace A., and Ripley, Randall B. *CETA: Politics and Policy, 1973–1982.* Knoxville, Tenn.: The University of Tennessee Press, 1984.

Gartner, Alan. *Paraprofessionals and Their Performance: A Survey of Education, Health, and Social Service Programs.* New York: Praeger Publishers, 1971.

Gartner, Alan; Carter, Vivian Jackson; and Riessman, Frank, eds. *Paraprofessionals in Education Today.* New York: Human Sciences Press, 1977.

Gartner, Alan; Nixon, Russell A.; and Riessman, Frank, eds. *Public Service Employment: An Analysis of Its History, Problems and Prospects.* New York: Praeger Publishers, 1973.

Georgetown University. *What Achieves Affirmative Action in Cities?* Washington, D.C.: Public Services Laboratory, Georgetown University, 1975.

Gittell, Marilyn; with Berube, M. R.; Gottfried, F.; Guttentag, M.; and Spier, A. *Local Control in Education: Three Demonstration School Districts in New York City.* New York: Praeger Publishers, 1972.

Glaab, Charles N., and Brown, A. Theodore. *A History of Urban America.* New York: The Macmillan Company, 1967.

Glazer, Nathan. *Affirmative Discrimination: Ethnic Inequality and Public Policy.* New York: Basic Books, 1975; Harper Colophon Books, 1978.

Goodnow, Frank J. *Politics and Administration: A Study in Government.* New York: The MacMillan Company, 1900; reprint ed., New York: Russell and Russell, 1967.

Gortner, Harold F. *Administration in the Public Sector.* New York: John Wiley & Sons, 1977.

Green, Philip. *The Pursuit of Inequality.* New York: Pantheon Books, 1981.

Hallman, Howard W. *Emergency Employment: A Study in Federalism.* University, Ala.: The University of Alabama Press, 1977.

Hofstadter, Richard. *The Age of Reform.* New York: Alfred A. Knopf, 1955.

Hoogenboom, Ari. *Outlawing the Spoils: A History of the Civil Service Reform Movement 1865–1883.* Urbana, Ill.: University of Illinois Press, 1961.

Horton, Raymond D. *Municipal Labor Relations in New York City: Lessons of the Lindsay-Wagner Years.* New York: Praeger Publishers, 1972.

Howard, Donald S. *The WPA and Federal Relief Policy.* New York: Russell Sage Foundation, 1943.

Lee, Robert D., Jr. *Public Personnel Systems.* Baltimore: University Park Press, 1979.

Levitan, Sar A., and Taggart, Robert, eds. *Emergency Employment Act: The PEP Generation.* Salt Lake City, Utah: Olympus Publishing Company, 1974.

Lindblom, Charles E. *The Policy-Making Process.* Englewood Cliffs, N.J.: Prentice-Hall, 1968.

Lowenberg, J. Joseph; Leone, R.; Koziara, K. S.; and Koziara, E. C. *The Impact of Public Employee Unions on the Public Employment Program.* Philadelphia: Temple University, Center for Labor and Manpower Studies, 1973.

McBain, Howard Lee. *DeWitt Clinton and the Origin of the Spoils System in New York.* New York: AMS Press, 1967.

McLaughlin, Lillie. *Detailed Statistics on Women and Minorities in New York State and New York City Government Employment: 1981–82.* Albany, N.Y.: Center for Women in Government, State University of New York at Albany, Spring 1983.

MacMahon, Arthur; Millet, John; and Ogden, Gladys. *The Administration of Federal Work Relief*. Chicago: Public Administration Service, 1941.

Martin, David L. *Running City Hall: Municipal Administration in America*. University, Ala.: The University of Alabama Press, 1982.

Mayers, Lewis. *The Federal Service: A Study of the System of Personnel Administration of the United States Government*. New York: D. Appleton and Company, 1922.

Mirengoff, William, and Rindler, Lester. *CETA: Manpower Programs Under Local Control*. Washington, D.C.: National Academy of Sciences, 1978.

————. *The Comprehensive Employment and Training Act: Impact on People Places Programs*. Washington, D.C.: National Academy of Sciences, 1976.

Mirengoff, William; Rindler, L.; Greenspan, H.; and Harris, C. *CETA: Accomplishments Problems Solutions*. Kalamazoo, Mich.: W. E. Upjohn Institute for Employment Research, 1982.

Mirengoff, William; Rindler, L.; Greenspan, H.; Seablom, S.; and Black, L. *The New CETA: Effect on Public Service Employment Programs: Final Report*. Washington, D.C.: National Academy Press, 1980.

Moscow, Warren. *The Last of the Big Time Bosses: The Life and Times of Carmine DeSapio and the Rise and Fall of Tammany Hall*. New York: Stein and Day, 1971.

Moses, Robert. *The Civil Service of Great Britain*. New York: Columbia University, 1914.

Mosher, Frederick C. *Democracy and the Public Service*. New York: Oxford University Press, 1968; 2nd ed., 1982.

Nathan, Richard P.; Cook, R. F.; Rawlins, V. L., and Associates. *Public Service Employment: A Field Evaluation*. Washington, D.C.: The Brookings Institution, 1981.

Nathan, Richard P.; Cook, R. F.; Rawlins, V. L.; Galchick, J. M., and Associates. *Monitoring the Public Service Employment Program: The Second Round*. Washington, D.C.: National Commission for Employment Policy, 1979.

National Academy of Public Administration. *A Review of the Philadelphia Civil Service System: Design for Accountability*. Washington, D.C.: National Academy of Public Administration, July 1981.

New York University Urban Research Center. *Wage Discrimination and Occupational Segregation in New York City's Municipal Work Force: Time for a Change*. New York: Urban Research Center, New York University Graduate School of Public Administration, August 1987.

Ostrom, Vincent. *The Intellectual Crisis in American Public Administration*. University, Ala.: The University of Alabama Press, 1973.

Pearl, Arthur, and Riessman, Frank. *New Careers for the Poor: The Non-Professional in Human Service*. New York: The Free Press, 1965.

Peterson-Hardt, Sandra, and Perlman, Nancy D. *Sex-Segregated Career Ladders in New York State Government: A Structural Analysis of Inequality in Employment.* Albany, N.Y.: Center for Women in Government, State University of New York at Albany, October 1979.

Pitkin, Hanna Fenichel. *The Concept of Representation.* Berkeley, Calif.: University of California Press, 1967.

Piven, Frances Fox, and Cloward, Richard A. *Regulating the Poor: The Functions of Public Welfare.* New York: Pantheon Books, 1971.

Rawls, John. *A Theory of Justice.* Cambridge, Mass.: The Belknap Press of Harvard University Press, 1971.

Rebell, Michael A., and Block, Arthur R. *Educational Policy Making and the Courts: An Empirical Study of Judicial Activism.* Chicago: University of Chicago Press, 1982.

Redford, Emmette S. *Democracy in the Administrative State.* New York: Oxford University Press, 1969.

Riessman, Frank, and Popper, Hermine I. *Up From Poverty: New Career Ladders for Nonprofessionals.* New York: Harper & Row, 1968.

Riordan, William. *Plunkitt of Tammany Hall.* New York: E. P. Dutton & Company, 1963.

Ripley, Randall B., and Franklin, Grace A. *Bureaucracy and Policy Implementation.* Homewood, Ill.: The Dorsey Press, 1982.

Royko, Mike. *Boss: Richard J. Daley of Chicago.* New York: E. P. Dutton & Company, 1971.

Ruttenberg, Stanley H. *Manpower Challenge of the 1970s: Institutions and Social Change.* Baltimore: The Johns Hopkins Press, 1970.

Salter, J. T. *Boss Rule: Portraits in City Politics.* New York: McGraw-Hill Book Company, 1935.

Sayre, Wallace S., and Kaufman, Herbert. *Governing New York City: Politics in the Metropolis.* New York: W. W. Norton & Company, 1965.

Schlesinger, Arthur M., Jr. *The Age of Jackson.* Boston: Little, Brown and Company, 1945.

Schweppe, Emma. *The Firemen's and Patrolmen's Unions in the City of New York: A Case Study in Public Employee Unions.* New York: King's Crown Press, 1948.

Shafritz, Jay M. *Position Classification: A Behavioral Analysis for the Public Service.* New York: Praeger Publishers, 1973.

Snedeker, Bonnie B., and Snedeker, David M. *CETA: Decentralization on Trial.* Salt Lake City, Utah: Olympus Publishing Company, 1978.

Spero, Sterling D., and Capozzola, John M. *The Urban Community and Its Unionized Bureaucracies: Pressure Politics in Local Government Relations.* New York: Dunnellen Publishing Company, 1973.

Stahl, O. Glenn. *Public Personnel Administration.* New York: Harper & Row, 1971.

Stanley, David T. *Managing Local Government Under Union Pressure.* Washington, D.C.: The Brookings Institution, 1972.

Stewart, Frank Mann. *The National Civil Service Reform League: History, Activities, and Problems.* Austin, Texas: The University of Texas, 1929.

Thompson, Dennis F. *John Stuart Mill and Representative Government.* Princeton, N.J.: Princeton University Press, 1976.

Thompson, Frank J. *Personnel Policy in the City: The Politics of Jobs in Oakland.* Berkeley, Calif.: University of California Press, 1975.

Truman, David B. *The Governmental Process: Political Interests and Public Opinion.* New York: Alfred A. Knopf, 1951.

Van Riper, Paul P. *History of the United States Civil Service.* Evanston, Ill.: Row, Peterson and Company, 1958.

Verba, Sidney, and Nie, Norman H. *Participation in America: Political Democracy and Social Equity.* New York: Harper & Row, 1972.

Viteritti, Joseph P. *Bureaucracy and Social Justice: The Allocation of Jobs and Services to Minority Groups.* Port Washington, N.Y.: Kennikat Press, 1979.

Waldo, Dwight. *The Administrative State: A Study of the Political Theory of American Public Administration.* New York: The Ronald Press Company, 1948.

White, Leonard D. *Introduction to the Study of Public Administration.* New York: The MacMillan Company, 1926; 4th ed., 1955.

Willoughby, W. F. *Principles of Public Administration.* Baltimore: Johns Hopkins Press, 1927.

Wirt, Frederick M. *Power in the City: Decision Making in San Francisco.* Berkeley, Calif.: University of California Press, 1974.

Wolff, Robert Paul. *Understanding Rawls: A Reconstruction and Critique of "A Theory of Justice."* Princeton, N.J.: Princeton University Press, 1977.

Young, Michael. *The Rise of the Meritocracy 1870–2033: An Essay on Education and Equality.* Middlesex, England: Penguin Books, 1961.

Zagoria, Sam, ed. *Public Workers and Public Unions.* Englewood Cliffs, N.J.: Prentice-Hall, 1972.

ARTICLES

Alford, Robert R. "The Bureaucratization of Urban Government." In *Social Change and Urban Politics: Readings*, pp. 263–278. Edited by Daniel N. Gordon. Englewood Cliffs, N.J.: Prentice-Hall, 1973.

Bagby, Thomas R. "The Supreme Court Reaffirms Broad Immunity for Seniority Systems." *Labor Law Journal* 33 (July 1982): 409–416.

Bartholet, Elizabeth. "Application of Title VII to Jobs in High Places." *Harvard Law Review* 95 (March 1982): 947–1027.

Bell, Daniel. "Meritocracy and Equality." *The Public Interest*, no. 29 (Fall 1972): 29–68.

Bernhardt, Herbert N. "Griggs v. Duke Power Co.: The Implications for Private and Public Employers." *Texas Law Review* 50 (May 1972): 901–929.

Browne, Constance A. "Absolute Veterans' Preference in Public Employment: Personnel Administrator of Massachusetts v. Feeney." *Boston College Law Review* 21 (July 1980): 1110–1142.

Cayer, N. Joseph, and Sigelman, Lee. "Minorities and Women in State and Local Government: 1973–1975." *Public Administration Review* 40 (September/October 1980): 443–450.

Couturier, Jean J. "Court Attacks on Testing: Death Knell or Salvation for Civil Service Systems?" *Good Government*, Winter 1971, pp. 10–12.

"Discriminatory Merit Systems: A Case Study of the Supervisory Examinations Administered by the New York Board of Examiners." *Columbia Journal of Law and Social Problems* 6 (September 1970): 374–410.

Eisinger, Peter K. "Black Employment in Municipal Jobs: The Impact of Black Political Power." *The American Political Science Review* 76 (June 1982): 380–392.

Gittell, Marilyn. "Putting Merit Back in the Merit System." *Social Policy* 3 (September/October 1972): 20–27.

Gordon, Daniel N. "The Bases of Urban Political Change: A Brief History of Developments and Trends." In *Social Change and Urban Politics: Readings*, pp. 2–18. Edited by Daniel N. Gordon. Englewood Cliffs, N.J.: Prentice-Hall, 1973.

Gould, William B. "Labor Relations and Race Relations." In *Public Workers and Public Unions*, pp. 147–159. Edited by Sam Zagoria. Englewood Cliffs, N.J.: Prentice-Hall, 1972.

Graham, Marcia. "Seniority Systems and Title VII—Reanalysis and Redirection." *Employee Relations Law Journal* 9 (Summer 1983): 81–97.

Greenstein, Fred I. "The Changing Pattern of Urban Party Politics." *The Annals of the American Academy of Political and Social Science* 353 (May 1964): 1–13.

Gross, Bertram M., and Kraus, Jeffrey F. "The Political Machine Is Alive and Well." *Social Policy* 12 (Winter 1982): 38–46.

Guinier, Ewart. "Impact of Unionization on Blacks." In *Unionization of Municipal Employees*, pp. 173–181. Proceedings of the Academy of Political Science, vol. 30. New York: Columbia University, 1970.

Hays, Samuel P. "The Politics of Reform in Municipal Government in the Progressive Era." In *Social Change and Urban Politics: Readings*, pp. 107–127. Edited by Daniel N. Gordon. Englewood Cliffs, N.J.: Prentice-Hall, 1973.

Hellriegel, Don, and Short, Larry. "Equal Employment Opportunity in the Federal Government: A Comparative Analysis." *Public Administration Review* 32 (November/December 1972): 851–858.

Ivie, Sylvia Drew. "Discrimination in Selection and Promotion of Minorities and Women in Municipal Employment." *The Urban Lawyer* 7 (Summer 1975): 540–555.

Jackson, Mike. "Racial Factors in Executive Selection." *Public Personnel Management* 8 (July/August 1979): 218–222.

Jones, James E., Jr. " 'Reverse Discrimination' in Employment: Judicial Treatment of Affirmative Action Programs in the United States." *Howard Law Journal* 25, no. 2 (1982): 217–245.

"Justice: A Spectrum of Responses to John Rawls's Theory." *The American Political Science Review* 69 (June 1975): 588–674.

Kaufman, Herbert. "Emerging Conflicts in the Doctrines of Public Administration." *The American Political Science Review* 50 (December 1956): 1057–1063.

Klingner, Donald E. "Political Influences on the Design of State and Local Personnel Systems." *Review of Public Personnel Administration* 1 (Summer 1981): 1–10.

Kranz, Harry. "Are Merit and Equity Compatible?" *Public Administration Review* 34 (September/October 1974): 434–440.

Larson, E. Richard. "Discriminatory Selection Devices in Public Employment Systems." *Good Government*, Winter 1971, pp. 1–12.

Lepper, Mary M. "The Status of Women in the United States, 1976: Still Looking for Justice and Equity." *Public Administration Review* 36 (July/August 1976): 365–368.

Lovell, Catherine. "Three Keys in Affirmative Action." *Public Administration Review* 34 (May/June 1974): 235–237.

McGregor, Eugene B., Jr. "Social Equity and the Public Service." *Public Administration Review* 34 (January/February 1974): 18–28.

Meier, Kenneth J. "Ode to Patronage: A Critical Analysis of Two Recent Supreme Court Decisions." *Public Administration Review* 41 (September/October 1981): 558–563.

Moses, Stanley, ed. "Planning for Full Employment." *The Annals of the American Academy of Political and Social Science* 418 (March 1975): ix–164.

Mosk, Justice Stanley. "Affirmative Action, Si—Quotas, No." *Employee Relations Law Journal* 9 (Summer 1983): 126–135.

Nagel, Thomas. "Equal Treatment and Compensatory Discrimination."

In *Equality and Preferential Treatment*, pp. 4–18. Edited by Marshall Cohen, Thomas Nagel, and Thomas Scanlon. Princeton, N.J.: Princeton University Press, 1977.

Nelson, William R. "Employment Testing and the Demise of the PACE Examination." *Labor Law Journal* 33 (November 1982): 729–750.

Nigro, Lloyd G. "Some Concluding Observations." *Public Administration Review* 34 (May/June 1974): 245–246.

O'Toole, Laurence J., Jr. "Doctrines and Developments: Separation of Powers, the Politics-Administration Dichotomy, and the Rise of the Administrative State." *Public Administration Review* 47 (January/February 1987): 17–25.

Panzarella, Robert. "The Impact of Tutoring Minority Recruits for Civil Service Exams for Police Officer Selection." *Review of Public Personnel Administration* 6 (Spring 1986): 59–71.

Pearson, James O., Jr. "Determination as to Good Faith in Abolition of Public Office or Employment Subject to Civil Service or Merit System." 87 ALR 3d 1165 (1978).

Rae, Douglas. "Maximin Justice and an Alternative Principle of General Advantage." *The American Political Science Review* 69 (June 1975): 630–647.

Renick, James C. "The Impact of Municipal Affirmative Action Programs on Black Representation in Government Employment: Reality or Rhetoric?" *Southern Review of Public Administration* 5 (Summer 1981): 129–146.

Rich, Wilbur C. "Bumping, Blocking and Bargaining: The Effect of Layoffs on Employees and Unions." *Review of Public Personnel Administration* 4 (Fall 1983): 27–43.

Risko, Paul K. "Recent Developments: Civil Rights." *Villanova Law Review* 26 (November 1980): 167–282.

Roberts, Robert N. "'Last Hired, First Fired' and Public Employee Layoffs: The Equal Employment Opportunity Dilemma." *Review of Public Personnel Administration* 2 (Fall 1981): 29–48.

Rose, Winfield, H., and Chia, Tiang Ping. "The Impact of the Equal Opportunity Act of 1972 on Black Employment in the Federal Service: A Preliminary Analysis." *Public Administration Review* 38 (May/June 1978): 245–251.

Rosenbloom, David H. "Public Administrative Theory and the Separation of Powers." *Public Administration Review* 43 (May/June 1983): 219–227.

Rutstein, Jacob J. "Survey of Current Personnel Systems in State and Local Governments." *Good Government*, Spring 1971, pp. 1–27.

Saltzstein, Grace Hall. "Personnel Directors and Female Employment Representation: A New Addition to Models of Equal Employment Opportunity Policy?" *Social Science Quarterly* 64 (December 1983): 734–746.

Savas, E. S., and Ginsburg, Sigmund G. "The Civil Service: A Meritless System." *The Public Interest*, no. 32 (Summer 1973): 70–85.

Schachter, Hindy Lauer. "Retroactive Seniority and Agency Retrenchment." *Public Administration Review* 43 (January/February 1983): 77–81.

Slack, James D. "Affirmative Action and City Managers: Attitudes Toward Recruitment of Women." *Public Administration Review* 47 (March/April 1987): 199–206.

Stein, Lana. "Merit Systems and Political Influence: The Case of Local Government." *Public Administration Review* 47 (May/June 1987): 263–271.

Urban Data Service. Andrew Boesel. "Civil Service Commissions in City and County Government." Washington, D.C.: International City Management Association, Vol. 5, No. 6, June 1973.

Van Horn, Carl E. "Evaluating the New Federalism: National Goals and Local Implementors." *Public Administration Review* 39 (January/February 1979): 17–22.

Van Riper, Paul. "The Administrative State: Wilson and the Founders— An Unorthodox View." *Public Administration Review* 43 (November/December 1983): 477–490.

Wicker, Christine, and Rosentraub, Mark S. "Affirmative Action and Local Government Employment: A Case Study of Institutional Response by Civil Service and Non-Civil Service Departments." In *Public Administration and Public Policy: A Minority Perspective*, pp. 317–333. Edited by Lawrence C. Howard, Lenneal J. Henderson, Jr., and Deryl G. Hunt. Pittsburgh: Public Policy Press, 1977.

Williams, Edward J., and Macy, James R. "Municipal Staff Reductions." *Wisconsin Bar Bulletin* 56 (February 1983): 12–15, 69.

Wilson, James Q., and Banfield, Edward C. "Political Ethos Revisited." *The American Political Science Review* 65 (December 1971): 1048–1062.

Wilson, Woodrow. "The Study of Administration." *Political Science Quarterly* 2 (June 1887): 197–222.

Wolfinger, Raymond E., and Field, John Osgood. "Political Ethos and the Structure of City Government." *The American Political Science Review* 60 (June 1966): 306–326.

PUBLIC DOCUMENTS

Griffenhagen and Associates. *Classification and Composition of the Service of the City of New York*. 4 vols. New York: Mayor's Committee on Management Survey, 1951.

Hoberman, Solomon. "Personnel Management and Labor Relations in New York City." In *Personnel Reforms for New York City*. State Charter Revision Commission. New York, January 1975.

Mayor's Task Force on City Personnel. *Report of the Mayor's Task Force on City Personnel*. New York, 3 May 1966.

New York City. Bureau of the Budget. *The City of New York Civil Service Commission: A Study of the Functions and Organizational Structure of the Civil Service Agency of the City of New York*. New York: The Bureau, 1951.

New York City. Department of Personnel. *Rules and Regulations of the City Personnel Director*. New York, 19 July 1978.

New York City. Mayor's Committee on Management Survey. *Modern Management for the City of New York*. 2 vols. New York: The Committee, 1953.

Richardson, Bellows, Henry and Company, Inc. *A Survey of Examination and Recruitment Procedures of the New York City Civil Service Commission*. A Survey Prepared for the Mayor's Committee on Management Survey of the City of New York, July 1951.

Sayre, Wallace S., and Kaufman, Herbert. *Personnel Administration in the Government of New York City*. A Report Prepared for the Mayor's Committee on Management Survey of the City of New York, March 1952.

Stanley, David T. *Higher Skills for the City of New York: Report of Study of Professional, Technical, and Managerial Manpower Needs of the City of New York*. Washington, D.C.: The Brookings Institution, March 1963.

State Charter Revision Commission for New York City. *Final Report of the State Charter Revision Commission for New York City*. New York, n.d.

————. *Personnel Reforms for New York City, Staff Recommendations*. Part I. New York, January 1975.

Temporary State Commission to Study the Organizational Structure of the Government of the City of New York (Josephs Commission). *Four Steps to Better Government of New York City: A Plan for Action*. 2 vols. New York: The Commission, 1953.

United States Civil Service Commission. *History of the Federal Civil Service 1789 to the Present*. Washington, D.C.: United States Government Printing Office, 1941.

UNPUBLISHED MATERIALS

Betsey, Charles L. "Minority Participation in the Public Sector." Washington, D.C.: The Urban Institute, November 1982. (Mimeographed paper.)

Cook, Robert F.; Galchick, J.; Maurice, A. J.; Orlebeke, C. J.; Rawlins, V. L.; Wiseman, M. L.; and Associates. *Public Service Employment in Fiscal Year 1980*. Princeton, N.J.: Princeton Urban and Regional Research Center, Princeton University, March 1981. (Unpublished material.)

Galchick, Janet M. "Administering Public Service Employment: The Effects of the 1978 CETA Amendments." Paper presented at the meeting of the American Society for Public Administration, Detroit, April 1981.

Gittell, Marilyn. "Evaluation of the Implementation of the Emergency Employment Act in New York City." Prepared for the National Manpower Task Force. October 1972. (Mimeographed.)

Gottfried, Frances. "The Myth of Meritocracy: A Study of Challenges to Municipal Civil Service Systems." Ph.D. diss., New York University, 1984.

Hoogenboom, Ari. "Outlawing the Spoils." Ph.D. diss., Columbia University, 1957.

Lemmey, William. "Bossism in Jersey City: The Kenny Years, 1949–1972." Ph.D. diss., City University of New York, 1979.

Saltzstein, Grace Hall. "External Pressures, Organizational Constraints, and Change: The Case of Municipal Affirmative Action." Paper presented at the Annual Meeting of the American Political Science Association, Chicago, 1–4 September 1983.

————. "Institutional Barriers to Representativeness in Bureaucracy: The Residual Effects of Organizational Reform." Paper presented at the Annual Conference of the American Society for Public Administration, New York, 16–19 April 1983.

Thompson, Frank J. "Meritocracy, Equality and Employment: Commitment to Minority Hiring Among Public Officials." Paper presented at the 1976 Annual Meeting of the American Political Science Association, Chicago, 2–5 September 1976.

Index

About the Author

FRANCES GOTTFRIED is Associate Dean in the School of Continuing Education at New York University. She served on the faculty of the Urban Studies Department of Queens College and the Political Science Department of Brooklyn College of the City University of New York. Dr. Gottfried is the co-author of *Local Control of Education*.